AF557789

MIRZA GHALIB

MIRZA GHALIB

a biographical scenario

GULZAR

RUPA

Published by
Rupa Publications India Pvt. Ltd 2005, 2011, 2025
7/16, Ansari Road, Daryaganj
New Delhi 110002

Sales centres:
Bengaluru Chennai
Hyderabad Jaipur Kathmandu
Kolkata Mumbai Prayagraj

P-ISBN: 978-93-7003-362-7
E-ISBN: 978-93-7003-231-6

First impression 2025

10 9 8 7 6 5 4 3 2 1

Designed and typeset by Arrt Creations, New Delhi

Printed in India

For
Mr. A.S. Tatari and Pt. Arun Kaul

CONTENTS

EPISODES

ACKNOWLEDGEMENTS

I must acknowledge with gratitude, the efforts of Sunjoy Shekhar, who did the first translation of this work more than a decade ago. The manuscript still retains a substantial part of his work, though I made many more changes in the script and the format later. I also acknowledge the efforts of Sanjana R.C., who has put her heart and soul, days and nights, and her smiles and tears in giving the final shape to this manuscript, inspite of her not being very conversant with the Urdu language. (My apologies for my desperate pestering). And finally, to my publishers for going out of their way to publish the original version also, with the same painstaking enthusiasm. I feel honoured that so far I am the only author they have published in Urdu.

FOREWORD

Ghalib towers above scores and scores of Urdu poets like a 'Victor' as his *nom de plume* suggests. He is as complex a poet as he is charismatic. His ghazals are unique, not only for the intensity of the emotions and thoughts they express, but also for their exquisite charm, and the profound feeling for the beauty of the world, which they reveal. Ghalib sang of 'all the phases of life'; his was a range and depth of feeling no other Urdu poet had. Given the captivating spell, semantic density and extreme quotability of his poetry, Ghalib today ranks with the best, and undoubtedly qualifies as a world-class poet. He is also valuable for a completely fresh approach to the world. He was endowed with a passionate appreciation of life, yet he deeply questioned the very fundamentals of faith and dogma, and brooded over the nature of joy and sorrow and life and death. He was endowed with an inquiring mind assailed by disturbing questions about the lot of man in this universe. He generally reveals a mood of melancholy, yet it is enlivened with a zest for life and love for 'ruby vintage' and 'foaming bowl'.

Interest in Ghalib's poetry has steadily grown in recent times. The modern mind is especially attracted by Ghalib's concern for ideas, subvertive interrogation, psychological probing, cryptic brevity, ingenious logic, and also by his capacity to flout the conventional poetic language. In Ghalib, the contemporary mind sees one who, like itself, is iconoclastic and cherishes the intellect while yet feeling the need for a spiritual center.

Today, we may ask whether is not the reception of Ghalib at the turn of the twenty-first century so pervasive and widespread that one may venture to say that Ghalib in India, perhaps, has already broken the language barrier and permeated the Indian literary mainstream? It would not be an exaggeration to say that Ghalib today is part of our collective memory as people of other languages too enjoy and quote him frequently. If one looks at the graph of the reception of Ghalib during the last century, the rise in recent times appears to be phenomenal. The role of the erstwhile gramophone companies, New Theatre of Bengal, and the advent of great singers, such as K.L. Sehgal and Begum Akhtar in the thirties and forties in this context is yet to be properly assessed. Most importantly, Sohrab Modi's movie on Ghalib (story by Manto, and screenplay by Rajinder Singh Bedi) contributed to spreading Ghalib's fame far and wide.

Then came the revolution of the electronic media with the advent of the audio and video cassette and the age of satellite television. Gulzar's highly sensitive serial, *Ghalib* entered this space and met the challenge of time at that critical moment. Jagjit Singh's singing and Naseeruddin Shah's characterization notwithstanding, Gulzar's creativity served as a *catalyst* in turning Ghalib into a household name in the subcontinent. There is no gainsaying that Gulzar immensely succeeded in identifying with Ghalib's complex and iconoclastic approach towards love and life. Today, he may justifiably claim that Ghalib had *three* servants; two died their natural death, *he lives on.*

The screenplay is being published after decades, which of course amounts to retrieving an historic and creative document. I hope it will be received with the love and care that it deserves.

Dr. Gopi Chand Narang
New Delhi
20 May 2004

PREFACE

'Ghalibiat' is in itself a complete solar system; wherein Ghalib himself is the sun and is surrounded by critics and researchers like planets! Some of who are important and some, well, aren't. Amongst them, one stands apart rich with oceans of knowledge – Dr. Gopi Chand Narang. At this point of time, there is none other than Dr. Narang who could be called an authority on Ghalib and Urdu. This scenario written by me is presented to him in utmost humility, in the hope that I would receive his valuable criticism, suggestions and corrections. I am grateful to him for his words.

I have a confession to make: I make no claims of authority on Ghalib or his works in its entirety. However, I do confess to having a deep bond with the poet. In school, I learnt Urdu from Maulvi Mujib-ur Rehman. It was thanks to him that I was introduced to great poets like Ghalib, Momin, Zauq, Nasikh and the other greats of the Urdu language. I experienced a kind of familiarity with Ghalib. Maulvi Saheb always addressed him as 'Chuchha Ghalib'! No other poet has thus been prefixed.

There are some elders with whom you form a bond that could be termed a friendship. While Maulvi Saheb used to teach us Ghalib, I could feel that warmth of friendship with the poet. I learnt Urdu only in school. After that, it was Hindi all along: Neither was it my age nor did I have the inclination to go back to the basics again. Maulvi Saheb left for Pakistan; the Urdu that he left behind, became a part of me. With time, my interest in Ghalib grew.

I always say Ghalib had three trusted servants who were always with him. The first was Kalloo, who was with Ghalib till his very last days.

The second was Wafadaar, who had a lisp. The third was I. They lived their time. I am still in service of him.

There was something 'down to earth' about Ghalib. The common man could identify himself with the poet. He was very fond of mangoes, on eating too many of them, he would get boils; he would then apply ointment and would describe the mundane details of applying it. He could have been your neighbour, so casual he was! I feel that I lived with Ghalib in his home.

He used to borrow money, on being unable to repay it, he would search for innovative excuses. I feel an emotional bond with him. I wish I could somehow repay all his debts. Instead, generations and I, we all owe a debt to him!

I don't know if anybody will agree with me or not, but in spite of having fathered seven children and none of them surviving, his sense of humour surpassed that of all the other intellectuals of his time. The thought of a second marriage never crossed his mind. He loved and respected his wife and shared the pain and loss of their children with her.

When 'Chuchha Ghalib' recited a couplet, it was from the heart; it was as though he had felt it. He had a vast repertoire of couplets for every turn that life took.

Ghalib was a gambler, but he played it like a game. He was fond of drinking and never tried to hide the fact. He was not ashamed of it. Nothing about him or his life else was 'put on'. No wonder, that his life left a deep impression on me. Whatever material I could gather on him over a period of ten or eleven years, I presented in the form of a serial on his life.

Now, did I make his life or did he make mine?

GULZAR
May 2004

one

I

THE NIGHT WAS YET to embrace the morning. Darkness hung in the air, though the sky had begun to change its hue, turning lighter at its edges. The street of Gali Qasim was wrapped in fading darkness. A few tattered curtains hung on some doors. Somewhere a goat, tethered to a threshhold, bleated timidly. A mosque stood silhouetted against the feeble attempts of the sun to fight the darkness.

"*Allah-O-Akbar*," the priest called the faithful to prayer.

"*Allah-O-Akbar*," echoed the numerous lanes and bylanes of Ballimaran.

The tattered curtains of a house shivered to life. A pair of aged feet in slippers crossed the threshhold of the house and turned into the street. The man tapped his walking stick on the road that led to the mosque, his heels pressed together. The *azaan* called the faithful: it was distinctly audible. The man kept to the path. The mosque stood in bold relief against his gaunt frame. He arrived at the foot of the stairs leading to the prayer quadrangle, removed his slippers, took the first step and then halted—the *azaan* was over.

A silence dropped from the dome of the mosque and engulfed the man. He turned his face and stared at the gate of the mosque. The gate was high and away. And aloof, looking almost condescendingly upon him. He looked fixedly at the gate, his eyes slowly moistened. His own voice was heard in recitation.

"Ye masail-e tasawuff ye tera bayaan Ghalib
Tujhe hum wali samajhte jo na baadaa-khwaar hota."

Ah Ghalib, the magic of your words and your ways with mystics!
you would have been a saint – if you were not addicted to drink.

He turned away, put on his slippers and began to walk back to his house. His own voice was heard again.

"Hu'e mar ke hum jo rusva hu'e kyun na gharqe darya
Na kabhi janaza uthta — na kaheen mazaar hota."

After death I was so digraced; why didn't I just drown in the river?
For then, no coffin had to be raised, nor any grave built.

Somebody crossed him in the street and saluted him, "*Adaab,* Mirza!"

He reached his house and parked himself on the stepstone outside.

A female voice enquired, "Come back, have you? You were up pretty early today, weren't you?" The voice seemed to be elderly. He did not respond. He kept tapping the ground with his stick, marking time.

The owner of the voice, his wife, peeped out from behind the curtains and looked at him.

She softly asked, "You didn't go then?" She was unable to mask her disappointment. Mirza merely shook his head. She paused and then admonished him, "There's still time. Go make your peace with Him."

Mirza answered but made no effort to be audible. His reply was more to himself, "Go? What face do I have to go before Him? He had been calling me for ages, for the last seventy years, calling me five times a day, but I was not amongst His faithful, dear. And now I am ashamed, not of Him, but of myself."

He looked away from his wife, away from himself, down the street. His eyes caught sight of a marble. He got up to pick it and rolled it in his fingers.

"What is it?"

"A marble," he showed it to his wife. "Must have slipped out of a little one's pocket. Come, want to play?"

"Marbles! You were too lost in playing with them when you carried me across this threshhold from my father's."

A mischievous grin flashed on Ghalib's face and his eyes twinkled. "That was the only way to win over the marbles that you had hidden, dear. Brought you over to the house, and the marbles too." He neared her, "Come, let's play." She rebuked him jovially, "Yes, this is all we need to do at our age!"

Mirza still had that spark of humour. He remarked, "As we do not have grandchildren to play with, why can't we play with this?" He caressed the marble between his fingers.

She suddenly seemed to be caught up in an avalanche of emotions. "Why do you blame me? With god's grace, I gave birth to seven children. If He did not will them to live, what can we do..." her voice seemed to come from an unfathomable depth.

He muttered, "You only blame Him...I didn't say anything. If I did not go and pay my homages, then I did not complain either..."

She turned and went back into the house. He kept looking at the curtain that did not allow a glimpse of her, with the marble still in his hand.

2

He marked a pocket on the ground and tried to aim the marble into it.

A man neared him, dressed in spotless white, a bright cummerbund shaped his otherwise flowing robes, with two equally spotless white pigeons in his hands. His moustache, sharp and imposing, sat comfortably on his upper lips, lending complacence to his gait. He raised his hand in a salute, "*Assalaam Aalekum*, Asad Mirza!"

Mirza returned his greetings, "*Walekum Assalaam!*" The pigeons looked out of the corners of their beady eyes at Mirza who instantaneously lowered his hand that held the marble. "Are these dancing pigeons?" he asked, mischievously.

"Where...where are those pigeons of Lucknow? Flew they all did, flew away since the advent of these *firangi* people..." a sense of regret crept into his voice.

"Why? Don't pigeons fly over the skies of Delhi?"

"Pigeons! Dirt flies over the skies of Delhi, Mirza Nausha, dirt! And the only other thing that flies away is the colour from the faces of the people. Go to the fort sometime, take a look at it, but you hardly ever step outside the confines of this street."

"Where shall I go? To which fort? Emperor Zafar no longer lives there...sent to Rangoon in exile by the Britishers; and the princes—their heads they hanged at the Khooni Darwaza! Whom shall I call my own in that fort now?"

"At least the Brits are there. Haven't they reinstated your pension? You must be glad, so what if the Emperor's not there?"

"Register your complaint not with me but with yourself, Mister. Nations are made not by the ruler but by the people. And had you not been flying pigeons today, this, our nation, would have been different, our country would have been better. Go put some wind beneath the wings of your pigeons!" Mirza's face displayed a multitude of emotions and a flicker of annoyance arched his brows.

The man's complacence seemed to be chipped and his face reflected hurt and humiliation. He turned and walked away, his hold on the pigeons slightly tighter. Mirza did not even look at his diminishing figure, nor did the walls of the houses of Gali Qasim. There was just a silence that spoke for itself. Mirza turned his attention to the marble.

And suddenly the lane brimmed up with the sounds of a song:

Sab nadia jal ....

"Rivers all bring offals of water to the sea..."

A blind fakir was singing, and led by a young girl, entered the lane at the far away end *"...and purge their souls with that offering."* They were almost at Ghalib's doorstep. He clanged his iron tongs together. The girl stopped as if the clanging of the tongs were a clue, and the blind man asked for the lady of the house, *"Maie...! Maie!"*

The sound of footsteps was heared from within and Mirza's wife, Begum Umrao appeared at the door of the house. She had a bowl of flour in her hand which she poured into the cloth bag that hung on the shoulder of the alms-seeker. Gratified, the man blessed Begum and moved on led by the young girl, still singing. The lane reverberated with his song. His sonorous tune clung onto the air of the lane. Begum called out for Mirza but he was oblivious to her beckoning, held captive by the song and the tune.

"This Brahmin sings very well," he said spontaneously and in appreciation.

"Won't you step in now?" Begum asked.

"What's there inside, Begum? A few empty bottles and some complaining wine glasses? That's all!"

"Shall I have them disposed then?"

Mirza shook his head in refusal.

"Go hathh ko junbish nahin, aankhon mein to dum hai
Rehne dho abhi saaghar – O – meena mere aagay."

"So what if my hands are robbed of the movement, my eyes still brim with life.
Let the bottles and the glasses be before me."

His voice had a strange note of loss and mischief.

"Come on in!" said the Begum, unable to mask her annoyance, "at least we have a home inside if not anything else, even wrecked would do!" She stepped inside with this outburst.

"Ghar mein tha kya jo tera gham usay gharat karta?
Woh jo hum rakhte the ik hasrat-e tamir, so hai."

"What did we have at our home that your sorrow could wreck?
All we had was a desire to create, and that is still there."

A coy smile broke out on Mirza's face and he took another position to aim the marble into the pocket.

3

A kaleidoscope of marbles fell with a jingle on the ground. A few youngsters were huddled together under the afternoon sun. One of them pointed towards a green marble and asked the pitcher to take a shot at it. The pitcher took aim and was about to shoot when another boy said, "Hold on! Move your feet ... yes, keep it on the mark ... yes, now shoot ... Wait ... Take a shot at the saffron one."

The boy took his aim and missed.

"Way apart!" another one shrieked in jubilation. "Your turn, Asad."

Asad bent down to gather the marbles scattered on the ground. An excitement gripped him and he dashed against an old man who was crossing the lane and fell.

"Can't you watch your steps, old fellow!" he shouted. The old man turned, offended at being addressed as old fellow. "You ... you little brat ... don't you know how to talk to your elders?" he nearly hissed.

"Buzurg ba akal ast na basal,"

Asad was unperturbed and quoted a verse in Persian, which took the man by surprise.

"What ... what did you say?"

"You have grown older, Mister, not an elder!" Asad translated the verse for the man's benefit.

The man, stung by Asad's rhetoric, stepped forward and pulled him by the ear. The gang of youngsters were silent spectators.

"What's your name?" the old man demanded.

"Asad Ullah!"

"Son-in-law of Illahi Baksh, aren't you? Where's your old man ... tell me?"

"You push me and then you ask for the address of my in-laws!" Asad replied, smarting in pain.

"Got a sharp tongue, haven't you?"

"Yes, a Persian tongue, do you understand it?"

The man went red with anger. He tightened his grip on Asad and dragged him to the inner courtyard of Illahi Baksh's home, all the while yelling, "Come ... let's go in ... let me tell your elders ... and then tell them that they are merely old people and not your elders..."

4

Illahi Baksh was engaged in a game of chess with Moulvi Samad Saheb. A chessboard was spread on a small table, a *hukka* on the side—long extinguished. The man coughed, "Maroof Miyan? May I come in?"

Illahi Baksh reclined on his chair on hearing the voice of the intruder, his eyes still glued to the chessboard. He took a few puffs at his pipe and realised that the *hukka* was out for long.

"Who? Ramzani?" he said, his words laced with humour, "Oh! do come in! In fact, you are already in!"

Ramzani goaded Asad in front of them. "Come on, tell them, tell them what you said."

Illahi Baksh looked up, this time managing to steal his eyes from the game spread in front of him. "What happened? Did Asad do something?"

"Opined that I have grown old, not elderly!"

Illahi Baksh looked in the direction of Moulvi Saheb who, like him, found it difficult to suppress a smile.

He asked, "Why, Asad Miyan did you say...?"

But before Illahi Baksh could cap his sentence with a question mark, Asad blurted out, "No, I did not say it...it was said by Sheikh Saadi, I merely quoted it."

Illahi Baksh and Moulvi Saheb exchanged another look. It was, however, Moulvi Saheb who questioned Asad this time, "What did Sheikh Saadi say?"

"He said:

'Buzurg ba akal ast na basal,
amir badil ast na bamal.' "

Both Illahi Baksh and Moulvi Saheb found it difficult to suppress their laughter. Their faces reflected their amusement.

Illahi Baksh took off the *chilam* from his hukka and asked Asad to get it afresh. He turned towards Ramzani and said, "No, Ramzani, I don't think that Sheikh Saadi said this for you."

Ramzani had already sensed that his complaint was not going to be addressed. He was now outwardly irritated. "Look, Miyan Illahi Baksh," Ramzani made no efforts to camouflage his irritation, "leave aside this fun and frolic and teach some etiquette to this brat or else...!"

The threat in Ramzani's voice rubbed Illahi Baksh the wrong way, "Or else? ... or else what will you do?"

"I will complain to the Nawab of Loharu," Ramzani said.

"The Nawab of Loharu is my elder brother," a smile broke on his face and sarcasm crept into his voice. "Why don't you go to the fort instead—the emperor is there and if he can't do anything about it himself, at least he will place your complaint in front of the British Resident..."

"Maroof Miyan, you are quibbling like young children do," Moulvi Abdul Samad intervened, and then turning towards Ramzani, said, "Miyan, you may go now. We'll see to it that Asad does not do anything of this sort again."

Ramzani left, muttering, "What do you expect from youngsters when their elders behave in this manner!"

Illahi Baksh once again directed his attention to the chessboard. He surveyed the chessmen and said, "Make your move, Moulvi Saheb!"

Moulvi Saheb did not react. As Asad returned with a lit *chilam,* he made his move and chuckled, "That's your very move, Sir!"

"Ok, now let me think!" Illahi Baksh was slightly uncomfortable.

"Run your knight, Chacha Jaan!" Asad whispered.

"But then he will take away my queen," Illahi Baksh had no faith in the advice rendered.

"Let him!"

Moulvi Saheb too was perplexed and looked questioningly at Asad.

"You try taking the queen..." there was a challenge in Asad's utterance.

"How come? Do you know how to play chess?" Moulvi Saheb questioned.

"You take the queen first and then I'll answer your question."

Illahi Baksh implemented Asad's advice, however reluctantly, baring his queen to Moulvi Saheb's attack. No sooner did Moulvi take the queen that Asad moved his castle. "Here, that's check and mate."

They were both taken aback.

"Wonderful!" Moulvi Saheb complimented Asad. "I did not even think of this move!"

Asad raised his hand acknowledging the compliment and left.

"That boy's a wonder. Whom did he learn chess from? You?" Moulvi Saheb enquired of Illahi Baksh.

"Me? Of course not!" Maroof let out a laughter. "Would he be making such smart moves were I his teacher? He learnt Persian in Agra from Moulvi Mouazzam and chess too—and at this age he recites and writes couplets in Persian and Urdu—aspires to become a great poet of Persian."

"Great! What nom de plume does he write under?"

"Asad!"

"And, where does he live? In Agra?"

"No! I brought him here. And he will live here now ... with me in Dilli."

They busied themselves in setting the game again. Moulvi picked up the threads of the conversation. "And who else lives in Agra?"

"Mother and younger brother—Yusuf Ali Khan..."

"And his father?"

"Long dead. Was employed in the service of the king of Alwar. Died in his service while out on a hunt. Thereafter, his uncle brought him to Agra under his stewardship."

"Wasn't he employed as subedar on behalf of the Marathas?"

"Yes, Sir, that's correct. Subedar of Akbarabad, perhaps. Yes, that's him. But when Agra was beseiged by the Britishers, his subedari was made into a commissonary and it was only last year that he fell from an elephant and died..."

He ran his eyes on the board and was intrigued by Moulvi Saheb's new move, "Oh! And what's this? I hadn't even dismounted my elephant that your knight has sharpened his lance."

Moulvi Saheb took his remark in good humour. "Shall we not try some new moves?" he said. Illahi Baksh made his move and suggested, "Do me a favour, Moulvi Samad Saheb. Take Asad under your tutorship. He is a sharp knight. Tutor him and you will have a crusader in your hands."

5

"Yes," Asad said, sitting at his desk on the floor, completing the last line dictated by his father-in-law, and dipping the nib of his pen into the inkpot, "what shall I write further?"

"Why don't you write it yourself, why ask me?" Illahi Baksh shifted his gaze from Asad's writing desk "Write that the pension agreed upon was ten thousand, which was chiselled down to half, half of which accrues to you and your brother, and the other half to Shams, your cousin. Now where has this Haji sprung from? Let Lord Lake understand that Haji is not a relation of yours and that he has unnecessarily jumped into the fray."

"I think," Asad commented with all the sense of a grown-up, "Haji and Shams are up to something."

"Fine! Write that, why don't you?" Illahi Baksh was visibly relieved. He stopped pacing up and down the room, picked up an old issue of a magazine and sat down on the diwan. He leafed through a few pages and then looked over the magazine at Asad penning the letter. He read aloud a couplet written under the nom de plume of Asad and commented,

"Iss jafa par buton se wafa ki
Mere sher shabash rahmat-e khuda ki."

"That's a rotten verse Asad, too rotten!"

"That's not mine!" Asad said, looking up from the draftsmanship, "This Asad is someone else."

"Too bad! All his rotten verses will be credited to you then."

"Yes, Sir, definitely," Asad added quickly, "and all my good ones will be credited into his account."

"I think," Illahi Baksh suggested, "you would do better to style a new nom de plume for yourself."

"I think I shall call myself Ghalib."

The name stuck a cordant note with Baksh. He repeated the name, over and over again, "Ghalib! Asad Ullah Khan Ghalib! Sounds good! But makes you appear pretty old. Conjures up a moustache and beard on your face."

"You like it?"

"Oh! I'll think it over, but you have to help me a little at that."

Asad looked up questioningly, "And of what help can I be?"

"There's a bottle in the almirah, go fetch it."

Asad got up with a smile. From an almirah in the wall, he took out a squarish bottle of whisky. He uncorked the bottle, and licked the cork to taste it. His lips turned up in disappointment. He brought the bottle to Maroof Miyan and asked, "Is this the bottle?"

"Bring me a glass too, dear, I wouldn't drink straight from the bottle, would I? And go tell somebody downstairs to roast some almonds and pistachios and have them sent up."

"Whom shall I ask?"

"Your wife, who else?"

"My wife! That teeny meeny girl. She'll roast her hands instead."

Maroof laughed heartily, "Goodness gracious! Started worrying about her a great deal, haven't you?"

Asad left the room once again. Maroof picked up the half-written letter and began reading it. A little later Asad entered, a cut glass tumbler balanced on his outstretched palm.

"Chacha Jaan!" he gingerly called out to his uncle, afraid that he would drop the glass, "there wasn't any wine glass, so she gave me this tumbler and said ..."

His words flagged off as he made an effort to steady the shaky tumbler.

"Careful, dear!" Illahi Baksh cautioned. And the glass fell with a thud on the floor and smashed into innumerable tiny fragments.

6

"Aur bazaar se le aae agar toot gaya
Saghar-e jam se mera jam-e sifaal achha hai!"

And you may fetch another if it may be ever broken
This, my earthern goblet, is better than the wine glass of Jamshed.

A bearded Mirza Ghalib stood looking out of the window, reciting couplets in *tarannum*. There was a youthful radiant glow on his face that may have belonged to a young man of twenty-five. The rays of the evening sun filtered in through the open window.

His wife entered and left a lamp in the room. He recited another couplet:

"Un ke dekhe se jo aa-jati hai mounh par rounaq
Woh samajhte hain ke beemar ka haal achha hai."

"And a glow appears on my face when I see her.
She gets the impression that I'm no longer ailing!"

Ghalib gathered his handkerchief in his hand in a knot and smiled. He walked towards the *diwan* and thought another couplet aloud:

"Dekhiye pate hain kya faiz buton se ushaq
Ik berhamin ne kaha hai ke ye saal achha hai."

Let's see what benefits do I get from idols of love
For a Brahmin has predicted that this year has good things in store.

And another:

"Hum ko maloom hai jannat ki haqeeqat, lekin
Dil ke khush rakhne ko, Ghalib ye khayal achha hai."

And though I know the truth about Paradise
What's the harm if I thus amuse myself.

He reclined against the *diwan* and shut his eyes.

two

I

A CARRIAGE DRAWN by a horse came to a halt in front of Ghalib's door. Bansidhar stepped down from the carriage. The coachman too jumped down from his seat to attend to his passenger. He inspected the exterior of Ghalib's house and casually asked, "Is this where Mirza lives?"

Equally casually, Bansidhar answered, "Yes." He moved to the back of the carriage and motioned the coachman to come near.

"Would you put that basket of vegetable down, brother?"

He picked up the basket and brought it to Bansidhar, "Here Sir, here's your basket." He again looked at the house and remarked, "Isn't this house much smaller than his Kalan Mahal in Agra?"

"Did you know Mirza in Agra?" Bansidhar asked.

The coachman smiled, placed the basket on Ghalib's doorsteps, brushed his hand against his dress and said, "Yes, Sir, I certainly did. You two snapped innumerable kites of Raja Balwan Singh. You and Mirza used to fly kites from the roof of Kalan Mahal and we used to wait for the strings to snap. We grabbed a lot of those rudderless things."

Wafadar, Mirza's maidservant, appeared at the door. She spotted Bansidhar and rushed to him. "Good morning, Sir!" she lisped a greeting.

"*Adaab* Wafadar! Is Mirza at home?" Bansidhar enquired.

"Dading a badh," (taking a bath) her reply had a well-pronounced lisp to it.

"Where is the Begum?" Bansidhar asked.

"In dhe inner shancduary. In convershadion widh dhe neighboursh."

"All right! Go tell her I've sent my salutations." She turned to go. Bansidhar called after her, "And ask Kalloo to keep this basket inside." She went in. He then turned towards the coachman, Biddu and said, "Biddu Miyan, there's an inn closeby. Unsaddle your horse there and park your carriage. Only tomorrow shall I go to Agra. Tonight I will stay here. At my friend's."

"Then shall I too stay at my daughter's? She's married here...in Dilli. I'll come for you in the morning..."

"That's fair!" Bansidhar said motioning him to come near. "Do one thing," he pointed towards the basket, "pick something from it. You must not go empty handed to your daughter's."

Biddu picked up a large gourd, profusely thanking Bansidhar. He hopped on to his driver's seat, bid adieu to Bansidhar and caught hold of the rein, clucked his tongue and turned his carriage. A manservant came out of the house, picked up the basket of vegetables and went in.

2

Bansidhar entered the house after him. Begum Umrao Jaan greeted him from behind a thin, laced curtain, "*Adaab*, Lalaji!"

"*Adaab*, Bhabhi!" Bansidhar replied. "How are you?"

"Greatness be to the Lord!" Begum said.

"And Mirza, how's he? You and your Dilli have so enchanted my friend that he has altogether forgotten that some of his dear ones live in Agra too."

"That's not true," she blushed, "only the other day he was remembering you."

"Has he found some way to the fort?"

Begum kept quiet, her eyes downcast. She kept clinging on to the border of the curtain.

"What's the matter, Bhabhi?" Bansidhar asked, "there's complaint in your silence."

"What shall I say? You are familiar with his ego and stubbornness. He would ask for credit from the grocer's but would not seek the help of his peers. Wouldn't wince even once while asking for a loan but God forbid if he has to live under anyone's gratitude. As long as father was alive we did manage to pull along. Now even he's gone..." suddenly a rich lush crept into her voice, "and the company he keeps nowadays—such wretches they are—intolerable. And such is his indulgence in drinks and gambling, whenever his pocket allows." She paused.

Bansidhar stood rooted to the spot. He lowered his eyes.

She added further, "And do not think that I'm complaining about my husband..." her voice was choked, "you are a childhood friend of his, little wonder that I shared my feelings with you."

Mirza appeared on the first floor. He put his hands on the railing of the balcony that opened out in the inner quadrangle.

"Bansidhar! So you have already held your court and heard the complainant! Where had you been all this while?" Mirza said in between snatches of laughter.

Bansidhar looked up and replied, "You didn't come over either. It's poor me who visited you twice."

The servant, Kallan, or Kalloo as he was fondly called, passed under the balcony with the basket of vegetables that Bansidhar had brought.

"What's this?" Mirza chuckled. "Why have you brought all these gourds and all, Lala?"

"Now ...now, mangoes do not grow all the year round..."

Begum butted in the friendly banter, "Please go up and make yourself comfortable, brother. I'll send some sherbet."

"Yes, come up," Mirza cajoled Bansidhar from the head of the staircase. Begum disappeared into the inner sanctuary and Lala began to climb up the stairs.

3

Mirza escorted him to his terrace room, offering an explanation to Begum's complaint, "Begum's complaint is just, Lala..."

"If it is just, why don't you do something about it?" They sat down on a *diwan,* a cushion propped against their sides.

"What shall I do? Tell me! Shall I stay at home?" Mirza paused. The pause seemed to stretch itself into an eternity. "You know, my first son was a still born," he continued, getting agitated, "and the second died within a few months of his birth. Begum's eyes are still moist with the loss. If I stay at home, I can't bring myself to see those eyes; whenever I see them, they seem to be in mourning. She was a believer right from the beginning, now she has begun to bury herself in prayers..."

Kalloo entered the room with a tray. He placed the glasses of sherbat and a plate of roasted cashews next to Bansidhar and went away.

"And how are you employed now?" Bansidhar asked Mirza.

"No hope of employment in the fort. Uncle's pension is stalled or better put, it's accumulating in the British account."

"Then how do you manage to pass your time?"

"A few hours every day is spent at Haji Mir's bookshop...some more with co-patriot gamblers at a game of dice. I throw the dice pretty adeptly, Lala, and the day I get to throw the dice of my fate, I'll win them all in my favour," Mirza replied.

Bansidhar picked up the sherbet and said, "When your father-in-law passed away, I thought you'd come back to Agra to your brother, but it seems you'll not leave Dilli now."

Mirza reclined against the pillow and appeared thoughtful and said almost instantaneously,

"Hai ab is mamure mein qahett-e gham-e ulfat Asad
Hum ne yeh maana ki dilli mein rahein khaenge kya?"

There's a dearth in this city of the pangs of unrequited love,
And though I am agreed to stay in Delhi what shall I feed myself on?

A smile twisted the corners of their eyes.

4

A few courtiers sat on *diwans* tastefully arranged on the floor. Sunlight invaded the room through huge arched windows that had their curtains gathered in a bunch. The room had an air of prosperity about it—expensive chairs cushioned with velvet, chandeliers on pedestals, a thick carpet on the floor.

Zauq, the owner of the house, entered the room, attired in gold brocaded silken robes, rings on most of his fingers, reciting a couplet:

"Garcha hai mulke Deccan mein in dinon qadr-e sukhan
kaun jaye Zauq per Dilli ki galliyaan chhor kar!"

Who will now leave these lanes of Dilli
So what if prosperity now camps in the Deccan!

The room burst with applause. Numerous voices said in unison, "*Wah-wah! Subhan Allah*!" One of Zauq's disciples sitting at a desk in the corner dipped his pen in the inkpot and said, "Encore, Ustad! Let me note it." Zauq looked in his direction and was reminded of something. "Miyan!" he addressed him, "what happened to the list of invitees that I had asked you to prepare for the *mushaira*?"

"It's ready, *huzoor*," the disciple answered. "I shall bring it to you in a moment." He came forward with a list and presented it to Zauq.

Zauq positioned himself comfortably on a chair and began examining the list. His brows knitted questioningly as he stumbled through the names of some new poets. "I see a few new names—and who's this gentleman—Asad Ullah Khan Ghalib?"

"Has come from Agra, Sir," his disciple answered, "lives at Ballimaran."

Zauq nodded his head in acknowledgement.

"From Agra? Asad ...Ullah...Khan Ghalib!" he let the full significance of the name seep in. Another courtier volunteered some more information on Ghalib's lineage. "His grandfather came to Hindustan from Samarkand... in the reign of Shah Alam. And spoke Turkish."

Yet another one added, "And his father, Mirza Abdullah Beg, was born here but he hardly spoke anything."

Laughter filled the room. Zauq merely smiled.

"And he?" he said, "what does he speak?"

"Believes himself to be a poet of Persian," someone supplied Zauq with the answer.

"Is he alone in his belief or do people believe it too?" Zauq was intrigued.

"Wants the Dilliwallas to acknowledge it."

"Asad...Ullah...Khan...Ghalib!" Zauq hummed his name.

5

A carriage awaited Bansidhar at the doorsteps of Ghalib's house. Biddu, the coachman, was there to attend to him. Ghalib and Bansidhar walked out of the house. They clasped each other's hands and then Ghalib tapped Bansidhar on his arm, "And Lala! Don't you come half-yearly here. Agra isn't that far away."

"I come here with the change of every season," Bansidhar said, "it's you who hardly ever comes that side."

"Will come now—once I get over this need to earn my daily bread—it's been ages since I've seen Yusuf Miyan," Ghalib tried to placate his friend's complaint.

"Asad, I'll reach your money safely to Yusuf, but there's something that I want to say..."

"What's the matter?" Ghalib coaxed, "yes, come tell me!"

"Look! My financial state is better now," Bansidhar said hesitatingly, "shall I leave some money with you?"

Ghalib kept his hand on Bansidhar's shoulder. His eyes moistened with gratefulness.

"Return it—whenever you may have it," Bansidhar added.

"And if I'm unable to?" Ghalib questioned.

"The money is all yours, either ways," Bansidhar said. "You'll only lighten the load off my pocket and conscience."

Ghalib patted him on the shoulder and said, "Look Lala—there are some people, lending money is their occupation; why unemploy them. And I haven't yet repaid the money I had borrowed for the kites and strings." He laughed lightly. A messanger broke into their conversation. He bowed to them and said, "*Adaab*, Sir!"

They both greeted him but were unable to place him amongst known faces. The man looked like an envoy of a wealthy person.

"I have brought a message for Janaab Asad Ullah Khan Ghalib," the man said and looked quizzically at Ghalib, "are you..."

"Yes," Ghalib said, "whom is the message from?"

"From the poet laureate Hazrat Mohammad Ibrahim Zauq."

Bansidhar and Ghalib looked at each other. Ghalib took the message scroll from him, unrolled and read it. He looked again at Bansidhar as he finished reading it.

The messenger asked, "Shall I wait for the reply, *huzoor*?"

"No," Ghalib said, "I'll have it sent."

The man left.

Bansidhar asked, "What does Ibrahim Zauq want?"

"Invited me to a *mushaira* at the fort, under the chairmanship of Prince Zafar."

Bansidhar's face beamed with happiness, tears glistening in his eyes. "Congratulations, my friend, my heartiest congratulations. You'll steal the show, I know."

6

Kabhi hum mein tum mein bhi chah thi
Kabhi hum mein tum mein bhi raah thi
Main wahi hoon Momin-e mubtila;
Tumhe yaad ho ke na yaad ho.

"There was an attraction between us once
There was a way between us once
We were lovers once
I wonder if you remember me
The one whom you used to count amongst the lovebirds
The one whom you used to call your faithful
I'm the same Momin the lover.
I wonder if you remember me."

The poet Momin, thus concluded his refrain. The hall echoed with applause, though the poem was only a love-poem it was easy for people to react to it.

A border of expensive woollen carpets hemmed the hall and the guests leaned against long upholstered cushions. There was such a profusion of chandeliers, candelabra, wall lamps, hanging lamps and Chinese lanterns that the hall was converted into a veritable dome of light. Everything was elegant, displayed good taste and in its appointed place. In the front, was a chief throne-like seat on which sat the presiding poet, Prince Zafar. The *shama*, a glass lamp with a flickering wick, was placed in front of the poet who had just concluded his poem. Ustad Zauq was seated next to Prince Zafar.

The prince pointed towards Ghalib and an attendant placed the *shama* in front of him to the sound of the announcement, "The light of the evening, the Shama-e-mehfil, is brought to Mirza Asad Ullah Khan Ghalib."

Mirza looked around once. A hush, laced with wonder at the newcomer, fell over the audience.

Mirza recited,

"Naqsh fariyadi hai kis ki shokhi-e tahreer ka
Kaghazi hai pairahan har paikar-e tasweer ka."

These signs are complaint to someone's endearing hand
Papery is the attire of all sizes of pictures.

There was no response from the audience. Ghalib recited the next line.

"Kave kave sakht jaani, hae tanhai na poochh."

Don't ask how rigorous are the pains of loneliness.

Mirza looked around expecting as it was wont of his co-poets to pick up his opening lines, his *misra,* but the silence continued. He was forced to request, "Pick up the *misra, hazarat.*" The silence remained unbroken. Finally, a man commented meekly, "I'm unable to pick it up. Too heavy it is." Another added with a hint of sarcasm, "Shall I enlist the help of a *coolie?*" The silence was broken with peals of laughter, not very loud but loud enough to reach the four corners of the hall.

The prince looked at Zauq who bowed his head.

Ghalib resumed, "I'll present my concluding couplet, the *maqta.*"

People reacted to his announcement.

The prince asked, "Mirza, you haven't concluded the *ghazal* as yet, have you?"

"Huzoor, I did not find a *coolie,*" Mirza politely answered.

Mufti, another poet sitting next to him asked, "Arrey, why are there just two couplets in your ghazal, Mirza, the *matla* and the *maqta*?"

"Please continue," the prince asked. Ghalib touched his forehead and recited his *maqta,* his last couplet.

"Bas ke hoon Ghalib asiree mein bhi aatish zeir-e-pa
Moo-e-aatish deeda hai halqa meri zanjir ka."

Alas! Ghalib, there's fire under your feet in this incarceration!
And, a hair burnt in the fire is the fetter to your shackles.

Nobody responded to his couplet. There was complete silence. Mirza quietly got up and left the gathering.

7

Wafadar opened the portals wide open at Mirza's knocking, a lantern in her hand.

"Greetings, *huzoor*," she said as she gave way to Mirza. "How was the *mushaira, huzoor*?" Her curiosity got the better of her.

A smile mellowed Ghalib's arched eyebrows into a smile. She hurried to catch up with Ghalib's brisk walk into the house and added, "You must have stolen the show. The king emperor...he...he must have capped your head with his crown."

Ghalib stopped for a moment and then resumed his walk across the verandah.

"Yes, he would have, had I only let him take off my cap." He halted once again, this time at the door to his wife's room and asked, "Is Begum in?" and barged into the room even before Wafadar could mouth the answer.

Begum was sitting on the bed, comfortably propped against the bed-post, engrossed in her knitting. Her gaze framed Ghalib against the doorway; her eyes questioning him. Though Ghalib had the answer, he preferred to keep his silence, forcing her to lend words to it, "How was the *mushaira*, at least tell me that?"

"No good!" Ghalib's slight shake of the head said it all. He looked at his wife, smiled and added, "Listen, ask somebody to fetch me my glass and whisky." He sat down by her side.

"A little disappointment and you run to seek solace in liquor and dices. These are the habits that do not find favour with me."

"You like me, don't you? Then why drag my habits between us?"

"It does not take long for love to change sides—I might just begin to hate you if the coin falls on the other side."

Ghalib's lips stretched into a smile and twisted the corners of his lips mischievously,

"Pila de oak se saqi, jo hum se nafrat hai:
Pyala gar nahin deta na de, sharab tho de"

Cup your hands to quench my thirst if you do so hate me
I ask not for the goblet, offer me wine at least.

With a frown on her face, Umrao Begum turned to her knitting, portraying disinterest.

Ghalib whispered, almost into her ears,

"Dikha ke junbish-e lab hi tamam kar hum ko
Naa de jo bosa, to mounh se kahin jawab tho de!"

Kill me with the tremor of your lips
I do not ask for a kiss, speak at least.

She chose to feel flattered by remaining annoyed and shouted for Wafadar.

"Yes, Begum!" Wafadar stood at the door at the Begum's command.

"Fix up Saheb's wine in the room upstairs."

Wafadar left and she turned to him, "Why don't you tell me what happened at the fort?"

"I would have told you, even exaggerated my achievements, but it's just my fate—nothing happened. Very decent folks, they don't even pick up a fight."

"The fact is that the Dilliwallas do not like you."

"Why? Is my face unshapely?"

"Unshapely be the face of your enemies. I was saying..."

The sound of glasses clinking reached the room. Begum cautioned, "Careful, Wafadar!"

"She hasn't broken the bottle, has she?" he asked Begum and she added, "Wafadar, ask Kalloo Miyan to arrange the drink. She's scared to enter your room. She says a devil camps there."

"She's right in her saying—is there a greater devil than I?"

"*Tauba! Tauba!*" Begum touched her ears, read an *aayat* and then turned to face Mirza. "It's better if we return to Agra. These Dilliwallas will not let you settle here."

Ghalib got up from the bed with a sigh and began pacing up and down the room, "Shia, Sunni, Hindu, Musalmaan—were not these divisions enough that people have now erected walls in the names of Dilli, Lucknow and Agra. This world seems too small to me, Begum, too small."

He stopped abruptly behind her and recited,

"Bazichay-e atfal hai duniya mere aage."

A child's playground is this world before me...

She looked up at him, a glow of pride on her face.

Ghalib smiled and hummed further, in *tarannum*,

"Bazichay-e atfal hai duniya mere aage
Hota hai shab-o-roz tamasha mere aage."

A child's playground is this world before me
Such feats occur every day and every night before me...

He tied a knot at one end of her dupatta and another as he hummed the next couplet,

"Ik khel hai Aurang-e Suleman mere nazdik
Ik baat hai aijaz-e masiha mere aage."

King Solomon's throne is an amusement before me,
The miracles of Christ just another thing before me.

The pride on Begum's face now burned bright in her eyes. She took the *dupatta* from Ghalib's hands and began putting knots as he recited more couplets and walked to the other side of the bed,

"Hota hai nihan gard mein sehra mere aage
Ghista hai jabeen khak pe darya mere aage

Mat pooch ke kya haal hai mera tere peeche
Tu dekh ke kya rang hai tera mere aage

Imaan mujhe roke hai, to khainche hai mujhe kufr
Kaaba mere peeche hai, Kalisa mere aage."

Expanses of deserts are mere patches of dirt before me
And in dirt rub the rivers their heads before me

Ask not what my condition is after you
See what's your colour before me.

If faith holds me back, disbelief tugs at me
The believers are behind me, the pagan before me.

three

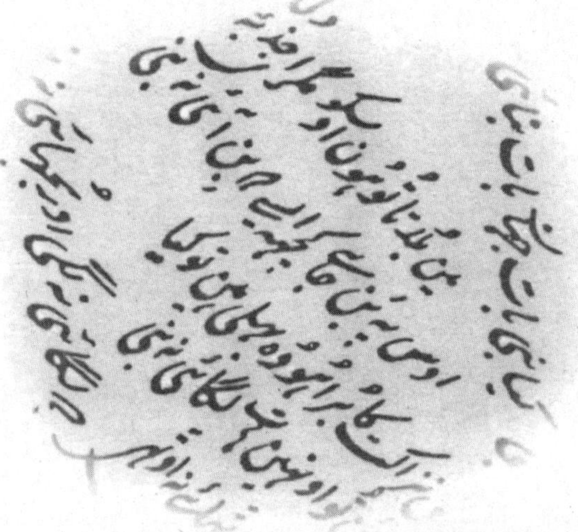

I

NAJMUDDIN, THE CALLIGRAPHER, dipped his pen in the inkpot and was about to write the couplet down from the manuscript spread in front of him. Numerous loose leaves of paper were sprawled all around him. He held a manuscript in his hands. He looked fixedly at it, dropped his pen in the inkpot and recited a couplet,

"Daem parha hua tere dar, par nahin hoon mein
Khak aisi zindagi pe ke pathhar nahin hoon mein."

I shall not be on your doorsteps forever
Be cursed such a life that I'm not a stepstone.

His face conveyed a respect for the lines recited. He read another one aloud,

"Kyun gardish-e mudam se ghabra na jae dil?
Insan hoon, pyala-O-saghar nahin hoon mein."

Why shouldn't the heart be fed up with ceaseless rotation of bad times.
A human I am, not a goblet of wine to be rotated around.

The couplets found their way to his wife's ears. She had her eyes on the stove where a mixture of dye and gum was kept on boil. She poked the fire, held the corner of the pan with the hem of her cloth and brought it over to him. She put the ink in the inkpot, watching her husband unable to control his joy as he recited yet another couplet,

"Yaa Rab, zamana mujh ko mitata hai kis liey?
Loh-e jahan pe harfe mukarer nahin hoon main."

Oh Lord! Why does this world erase me
I'm a letter that cannot be rewritten on the slate of life.

"What a thing to say, wonderful," Najmuddin was a bundle of ecstacy. "I'm a letter that cannot be scribbled again on the slate of the world—Oh Lord, why do you erase me? Why friends, why do you erase him—"

His wife could curb her curiosity no longer, she asked, "Who's this gentleman whose poetry has thus captivated you?"

"Who else can it be besides Mirza? Who else can write such poetry?"

"Who Mirza?" she asked, irritated.

"Mirza Ghalib!"

She caught her head in her hands, "Oh! Lord! Whose assignment have you brought! Not a single *cowrie* will you get from him—let alone your calligraphy and styling, you will not even get enough to pay for your pens and ink—indebted to the whole of Dilli he is, don't you know?"

"Wait till this anthology is published, Begum! The whole age shall be indebted to him—such poets are not born so easily..."

"Yes, and they also do not die so easily," she got up muttering under her breath. "Have you some money to run the kitchen?"

He put his hand in his pocket and said, "Only the other day I gave you a rupee."

"So do you expect it to last for a month?" she grumbled.

"If not for a month, at least for a week. Be a bit economical." He gave her some change and she left him to his work and poetry.

2

The poets were gathered at Prince Zafar's palace.

"Abu Zafar hasn't come yet," Zauq said to an impatient Mufti.

"I'll take your leave, it may be quite late by the time he arrives," Mufti argued in favour of his departure.

"What's the hurry, Mufti Saheb?" Momin asked, a part of his chest visible through a slit in the flap of his wine-coloured tunic, a deep purple sash folded into a girdle around his waist, with the two ends hanging in front.

"I think I should better go visit Mirza Ghalib. The other day he had walked out of the *mushaira* in a huff," Mufti explained.

"Oh! You need not worry your head over that," Momin said, "he must be happily engaged in tying and untying knots somewhere."

"Bhai, tying knots would mean that he's reciting his couplets," Zauq commented, "what would untying the knots signify?"

"Sheikh Sa'ab," Momin addressed Zauq, "a peculiar habit does this man possess. Recites couplet and puts a knot on a piece of cloth, he does. And the next morning, he unties each knot and notes the couplets down."

"Bhai, he does have a wonderful memory, but does he also have talent?" Zauq enquired.

"I'll take your leave. God be with you!" Mufti walked out of the room leaving Zauq's question unanswered.

Zauq turned to Momin who was adjusting the delicate lace at the edge of his cap that now clearly revealed the parting on his forehead, "Miyan Momin, has any anthology of Ghalib's been published?"

"Not to my knowledge," Momin said and again readjusted his cap that was capacious enough to sit comfortably over his head.

3

Mufti Saheb arrived at Ghalib's house and was surprised to see him feeding a kitten. He asked, "Come on Mirza, what is this love for pets?"

"No, not I Mufti Saheb, I am interested in pets," Ghalib was walking slowly with a bowl filled with milk to the brim, engaged in conversation with Mufti who sat smiling on the terrace. "Remember that friend of mine from Agra—Bansidhar? Last time I had asked him not to bring baskets of gourds anymore, so this time he brought me this cat." He sat down on his haunches and placed the bowl before the cat who started lapping it up hastily, spilling milk over the edges. He got up, still talking, "His cat gave birth to six kittens this time. He brought the loveliest of them for me. Now, if he wishes to share his kids with me, how am I to refuse..." By now they had joined Mufti Sadruddin on the terrace. "And then he said that the cat like me, was hooked on to meat, but it would hunt for itself, thereby making it necessary for me to house rats."

Mufti laughed and remarked, "If there are sacks of grains in the house, god willing, there shall be no dearth of rats."

"Yes, I fear the will of the Lord. I am afraid that there may be a dearth of grains."

Mufti got up with saying, "I'll take your leave Mirza, I better make a move."

"Do come again," Ghalib requested.

As Mufti began climbing down the stairs, Ghalib cautioned Mufti, "Careful, Mufti Saheb! The stairs are a bit steep," and followed him down to the door.

Before he stepped out of the doorway, Mufti turned and asked, "What happened to your anthology, Mirza, the one that Bansidhar was supposed to have got printed from Lucknow..."

"It's at the calligrapher's. Been there over two months now. He must be about to finish it. Perhaps a day or two more. I'll have it picked up thereafter."

Mirza bid adieu to Mufti at the door, "God be with you, *Khuda Hafiz*!"

"God be with you!" Mufti echoed his sentiments.

The calligrapher appeared at the door within moments of Mufti's departure, "Greetings, Mirza Nausha!"

Mirza turned around and with surprise in his voice said, "You've got a long life, Miyan! I was just talking about you to Mufti Sadruddin."

"I've completed your *diwan, huzoor*!" He placed the anthology on the plinth immediately outside the door and flipped the pages of the book to show Mirza his craftsmanship.

"*Huzoor*!" he said, "I'm too small an entity to possess any intellect to comment on your poetry, but I must let you know that you are a great poet—your couplets are like rivers in spate confined in a well—I am absolutely mesmerized by them."

Elated, Ghalib brought out some coins from the folds of his sash and offered them to the man saying, "I had asked you to write the anthology, not to read it, *Miyan!* This is your remuneration for writing it and you owe me some for reading it."

"Of what good am I, Sir—but let this be." He refused to take the offered coins.

"No, *bhai,* you have repaid me enough with your appreciation, let me pay you for writing it," Ghalib persisted.

"Mirza, this is a bit too many," the calligrapher registered his reluctance.

"Go spend some and it will be reduced," Ghalib forced the coins in his hand. The calligrapher left after paying his respects, and Mirza was engulfed in the innards of the house.

4

The curtain froze everything into a silence.

"Kalloo Miyan!" Mirza called for Kalloo as he came in, "fetch me that balm, my head feels a bit heavy."

Kalloo came in beaming. He paid no heed to Mirza's request, tiptoed near him and whispered, "Congratulations, *Huzoor!*"

"What! Are you congratulating me on the heaviness of my head?" Ghalib retorted.

"*Huzoor;* your head's heavy and Begum's feet! Wafadar told me—Begum meant it to be a secret!"

Mirza couldn't contain his excitement. He dipped his hand in his pocket and brought out a handful of coins. He thurst them in Kalloo's hands.

"This is your reward for the good news." Saying this he headed straight for the Begum's bedroom.

5

Reaching the bedroom Ghalib called out softly, "Begum!"

She hurriedly hid something under a long upholstered cushion and wiped her mouth with her dupatta.

"What's that you are nibbling at?"

She blushed.

"Will you not share it with me?" Ghalib questioned.

"Uh-hum!" she vehemently shook her gead.

Mirza came and sat down near her, "You must share it with me."

She covered her mouth and said in a muffled tone, "I'll be back in a moment." She almost ran out. Mirza pulled out a cake of *gachni mitti* from under the pillow and loudly said, "Oh ho! So it is *gachni mitti* that you have been eating!"

Begum rushed back into the room and snatched the cake away from him,

"God! This is imprudent of you."

Mirza looked into her eyes and smiled, "The imprudency was mine...that now limbs are being formed!"

"What language!" Begum reddened.

"But why didn't you tell me—why did you keep it a secret from me?"

"It would have been embarrassing for me," she bashfully said.

"And isn't it embarrassing sinking your teeth in this cake of *gachni mitti*. Think what your father, god bless him in heaven, would have done to me had he seen you feeding on clay. When the ladies of the nobility are expecting..."

"Softly! Speak softly, Kalloo is at work outside, he may hear us," the Begum said.

Mirza let out a roar of laughter. "He won't dare. He hadn't listened even when he gave me the news—kept his hands on his ears when he told me."

"Oh God, Oh God! So this has to be the garrulous Wafadar, can't keep anything secret."

Mirza called, "Kalloo Miyan! Would you please come in?"

"What are you calling him for now?" Begum enquired.

Kalloo appeared at the door, "*Huzoor*, you called me?" He had a pleasant smile on his face even though his eyes were downcast, a scarf hung on his shoulder, the money securely tied in one corner.

"Kalloo Miyan!" Mirza said, "fetch a few baskets of green unripe mangoes from the bazaar for Begum!"

Begum pinched Mirza quietly. Kalloo who stood at the doorway with his head bowed and said, "The mangoes haven't blossomed yet, *huzoor*!"

"Why, Kalloo Miyan, I heard the koel this very morning."

"Must have cuckoed with expectation, Sir!"

"Wullah! You have used 'expectation' beautifully, Kalloo Miyan!"

Kalloo acknowledged the compliment, "It's your greatness, *huzoor*!"

"Then why don't you get home a few sacks of almonds and pistachios?"

"A few sacks?" Begum reacted.

"An art it is to ask for credit, Begum!" Mirza turned to her, "ask for a sack and you get only a bagful."

"All this credit—how do you plan to repay it?"

"Wait till the verdict comes—the pension that's accruing with the government on account of our father's and his brother's estate shall all be reimbursed and then we shall buy bazaars Begum, not just shops."

He looked at Kalloo who was still standing with his head bowed, "Go, Kalloo Miyan! Go! Though the bazaar doesn't acknowledge my poetry, it does my credit-note."

His eyes followed Kalloo's receding figure.

6

Wafadar assembled all the small bags of her purchases at the grocer's into a big cane basket of fine weave. The grocer looked intermittently from the jottings he made in his notebook, his *bahi khata*, then at her, listening to her incessant talk in snatches, "It's just a matter of a few days—the government is about to restore Mirza's estate..."

A fakir came to the shop with a boat-shaped bowl, a fire lit in its midst, and sought *khairaat*. One of the men sitting around the shop put a coin in his bowl and hurriedly turned towards Wafadar, lest he lost track of the conversation.

"The estate in Agra? The one that belonged to his uncle?" he asked.

"Yes, Sir," Wafadar replied.

"Will he return to Agra then?" another asked. The conversation had generated enough interest, enough to divert their attention from the *tamasha* of the bear that filled the emptiness of the otherwise quiet bazaar; loud enough to be heard in the otherwise lonely bazaar; loud enough to be heard above the din of the dull sound of the *dugdugi*.

"Why must he go to Agra?" Wafadar was annoyed. "He will become the poet-laurete, here at the fort. It's just a matter of a few days."

"A few days!" yet another butted in. "They say something else at the smokehouse—that Mirza would have been better riding a horse than writing poetry."

People burst into laughter. Wafadar's face broke into a frown and she fumbled around with the knot at the end of her palloo. She finally untied it and gave a jingle of coins to the grocer, "Put this money into Mirza's account."

Before the laughter could ebb away, someone again remarked, "He's good at everything but his verses."

"He throws dice too, and pretty styishly," another remarked.

"Yes, and if this continues, he'll soon be diced to dirt," a voice further said.

Wafadar left the shop without waiting for the laughter to subside.

7

Mirza scooped up the dice, cupped them in the palm of his left hand and rolled them on the *chausar* with a final shake of his hand.

One of the four people who were playing dice on the verandah remarked, "Fate's your mate today, Mirza—your winnings are sizeable."

"When did I lose, Nadim Miyan? They say a loser in love is a winner at dice."

A man hastened to inform, "Saadiq Saheb, fold up your game...fast...hurry," the urgency became transparent, "the Kotwal's on his way..."

Sadiq started wrapping the *chausar* to Ghalib's surprise, "Why? Why? What happened?"

"Get up, Miyan," said Saadiq with the same urgency as the informer, "you'll be caught otherwise, the Kotwal will be here any moment."

"So let him come, let him try his hand at the game. Does he play better than us?" Mirza said with a smile.

"You will be packed to the gaol if caught," Ghalib's utterance offered puzzlement to the newcomer, "aren't you aware it's illegal to gamble?"

The Kotwal entered the street on horseback. A few passersby raised their hands in salute. Ghalib was stepping down the verandah of the house as the Kotwal approached him.

He asked, "What's happening, Mirza?"

"We were gambling and your arrival spoilt the fun."

"Gambling is prohibited by law, you know that, don't you?" the Kotwal adopted a friendly tone.

"Even if one gambles with his own money?" Mirza was nonplussed.

"Yes, it's illegal even if you play within the confines of your own house," the veneer of friendliness withered at its edges.

"What people are upto in their houses, even angels cannot know that, Kotwal Saheb!" Ghalib teased.

"The devil does come to know about it, Mirza! We have a list that spells out the names of all the gamblers." Friendliness had altogether disappeared from the Kotwal's tone.

"Mine too?" Ghalib enquired

"Yes, Sir, yours too."

Mirza found it difficult to suppress a smile and said,

"Chalo zikr mera mujh se behter hai ke us mehfil mein hai."

The mention of me is better than I,
for it's in your august gathering.

Saying this, Mirza ambled. The Kotwal jerked his head and watched the flowing robes of Mirza balloon up with the wind. His eyes spoke of some sinister resolve that had slipped from his mind into his heart.

8

The dawn lit up the lane of Gali Qasim with its bunch of hopes and disappointments safely tucked in its bosom.

A saintly figure turned into the street singing,

"Patta, patta, boota, boota, haal humara jane hai
Jane na-jane, gul hi na jane, baagh to sara jane hai."

Every leaf and every twirl knows the state of my being
Only the blossom doesn't though the entire garden does.

"A very lively couplet, Hafizji!" Mirza approached the man. "Who has penned it?"

The man blinked. "It's Mir Taqi Mir's. Belonged to Dilli, he did."

"Does he have a way with words!" Ghalib marvelled and said to himself,

"Rekhtah ke tumhi ustad nahin ho, Ghalib!
Kehte hain agle zamane mein koi Meer bhi tha."

You are not the only master of the language, Ghalib
There was a Mir in the age gone by.

He lowered his tone mischieviously and whispered in Hafiz's ears, "Recite it at the door of Hazrat Ibrahim Zauq, let it be known to him that a twist of phrase and a turn of rhyme do not constitute the art of verse. I'm a lover of good poetry. Wherever I may find it, whosoever the person may be." Saying this he fished into the folds of his sash and emptied all the contents into the man's bowl.

"God bestow a long life on you, Mirza!" Hafiz blessed him and moved away singing.

The street vibrated with life at his song.

"Patta, patta, boota, boota, haal humara jane hai
Jane na-jane, gul hi na jane, baagh tho sara jane hai

Charah gari bimar-e dil ki rasme shaher-e husn nahin
Warna dilber-e-nadan bhi is dard ka chara jane hai

Mehro wafa lutf-O-enayat ek se waqif een mein nahin
Aur tho sab kuch tazo kenaya ramzo ishara jane hai."

four

I

ROWS UPON ROWS OF glittering earthen lamps lit up the night with hope.

Outside Har Gopal Tufta's house, a little girl held out a tray of earthen lamps for another who would pick them up one by one and place them in a row beside the wall. A few men looked amusedly at them from inside the house. Ghalib, Tufta and a few others were engaged in a game of black gammon. Ghalib threw the dice to a winning combination once again, against the faint recitation of mantras glorifying the worship of Lakshmi, the goddess of fortune and prosperity, that came from the inner courtyard of the house.

"Ustad!" Tufta said, "you win at every Diwali!"

"Bhai Har Gopal Tufta," Ghalib said, "I'd have won at Id too, only it is not ritualistic to play then."

"Id isn't far away, they would be celebrating it in the next fortnight," someone chipped in.

"When did you let rituals and customs hold you down, Mirza?" another remarked.

"Don't say so, *bhai.* I have faith in all rituals, perhaps that's why I do not adhere to any single one and of all customs that are in vogue—even though they may not be rightful, like someone's else's poetry is in vogue at the fort."

Laughter escaped Tufta and took the entire gathering in its folds.

The incantation of the divine diety that weaves a magical background to the gathering ended. The priest entered the room and went around putting tilak on the foreheads of the men with a paste of sandalwood and vermilion from a platter that also held a lit lamp. He bypassed Mirza. People placed coins on the platter as an offering to the diety.

"*Purohitji,*" Mirza said, "though I may not worship Laxmi, I have admiration for her. Put tilak on my forehead too, desperately do I need her blessings."

The *purohit* dipped the tip of his ring finger in the paste smiled, halted and put a tilak on Mirza's forehead. He too, like the others, put some coins on the platter.

"You look handsome with the tilak on your forehead, Mirza Nausha!" one remarked.

"Yes, a Hindustani to the hilt. In my childhood, I used to land up at Bansidhar's home at every festival to gorge myself with *puris* and used to look more Hindu than Bansidhar with the *tilak* on my forehead."

Ghalib had barely completed his sentence when Har Gopal's young son barged into the room. He had an *anaar* (firecracker) in his hand. "*Pitaji,*" he addressed his father, "light my *anaar* for me."

"Light it for yourself and let me play," Hargopal said.

"*Miyan* Tufta," Ghalib intervened, "why don't you help the little one?"

"You've had your turn, why don't you?" Tufta said.

"Let's go, Miyan Pitamber Singh," Ghalib stood up, "come, I'll light it for you."

The smile returned on the young one's face and they walked out of the room, hand in hand.

"Lo!" Tufta sighed with relief, his undivided attention once again on the game. "The kids are taken care of by Chacha Ghalib."

Outside, brilliant fireworks traced mythical legends in a dark black sky and the flames of the lamps leaped to match its might with the illuminated sky. Ghalib walked, still hand in hand with the tiny tot to a group of children dancing in glee at the bursts of the crackers. He placed the *anaar* on the ground and asked for matches. The kid placed a colourful matchbox in his hands. He rustled the box open and lit the *anaar,* when an old fond memory leaped up from inside his heart and lit up his face.

On the terrace of a house in Agra, young Asad was engaged in conversation with little Umrao.

"Umrao, light the *anaar*! Go light it—Bansidhar, let Umrao light it."

Bansidhar, resplendent in festive garments with a *tilak* on his forehead, beckoned Umrao.

"I'm scared," Umrao said to Asad, to Bansidhar and to the rows upon rows of dancing flames.

"Afraid! What of? Aren't we here?" Asad offered encouragement.

Umrao looked at the sparkler, at Bansidhar and then turned her gaze at the rows of lit lamps which seemed to ridicule her fright. She tiptoed to the *anaar*, her dupatta dragging on the ground.

Asad stealthily tied a few crackers on the edge of her duppatta and lit it.

"Aa...ammmi..." A startled and scared Umrao shrieked for her mother. She threw her dupatta and ran away.

Asad and his friends laughed their hearts out.

Bubbles of firework oozed out of the *anaar's* mouth and it soon formed a fountain of light, bursting high, sky high.

Mirza stepped back a little and stood with the other children watching the fireworks.

2

Mirza walked back into his own street—Gali Qasim. A few houses had lamps lit on their terraces. Here and there, a few children were engaged in lighting crackers. As Mirza neared his house, two servants rushed up to him, greeted him and placed a box of sweets in his hands.

"Salaam!" Mirza greeted. "Yes, Chandan, Sukhanandji has sent sweets, hasn't he?"

"Yes, Sir!" Chandan answered.

Ghalib took out a few coins and tipped them both, "Convey my thanks and greetings to him." They left.

As Ghalib was about to enter the house, Ramzani who stood a little away approached him and said, "Mirza—you'll feast on the sweets of Diwali, will you?"

Mirza opened up the box of sweets, peeped at its content, smiled and said, "Here's some *burfi,* will you have some?"

"Aren't you a Mussalman...?" Ramzani's religious pride seemed to be offended.

"And burfi—is it Hindu?"

"What else? Tell me?" Ramzani stared at him.

Ramzani growled.

"And *jalebi*? Which religion and caste does it belong to—Khatris? or Shia? or Sunni?"

Ramzani walked away in a huff. Mirza looked at his departing figure and laughed as he climbed the step to his house, muttering:

"Bana kar faqeeron ka hum bhes, Ghalib!
Tamaasha-e-ahele-karam dekhte hain."

3

"The verdict on the pension, Asad Bhai," Shams said as he walked a few paces with Ghalib towards the chairs, "will take time, the whole affair is in the hands of the British—from the resident to the commissoner, from the commissoner to the governor, from the governor to the governor general. Quite possible, they may send us packing to Queen Victoria."

Ghalib listened intently to his cousin, his hands clasped together and said as they walked out of the verdant green mango grove of the inn, "I've heard you have learnt English, Shams, why don't you make them understand?"

"Yes, No, Yes Sir, No Sir—that's all I had learnt, but these foreigners are crazy—they speak fluent Urdu and Frazer has even found a tutor......"

"Frazer?" Ghalib questioned, "who's this Frazer?"

"At present, the commissoner of Dilli and I believe he is to become the resident soon."

"Have you met him? What did you say his name was?"

"William Frazer! Yes, I have met him. He said...said that the whole matter from the beginning till the end must be given to him in writing—so that he may send it to the governor general—the verdict can only be made thereafter."

They neared the chairs laid out under a mango tree where wine had been laid in decanters. Two horses, well-groomed and majestic, were tied by their reins to a tree. Shams took the decanter and poured himself a drink.

Ghalib asked as he made himself comfortable in a chair, "So, have you got it petitioned or shall I write it down?"

"I have asked Haji Khawaja to prepare the papers," Shams said.

"But doesn't Haji treat himself as a partner in the entire argument?"

Shams stopped him with a gesture and whispered in a tone laced with secrecy, "Asad Bhai, let the work be done for now, we will sort that out later—he is doing all the running around, after all." Haji sauntered into the picture, as if on a cue, with a thickset of papers and raised his hand in greeting, "Taslim, Mirza Nausha!" Ghalib nodded his head indifferently, making it quite obvious that he did not like the person. Shams, however, poured a drink for Ghalib and offering it to him said, "Frazer had assured us that he will talk to the resident and provide us with a grant from the royal treasury..."

Ghalib rejected the offered glass, "No—I don't drink during the day!"

"Good liquor, brewed here in Mehrauli itself," Shams insisted.

"Mirza Nausha," Haji who was still standing said, "only drinks alcohol brewed in Scotland—Old Tom bought from Meerut Cantonment."

"Must be pretty expensive!" Shams remarked.

"Yes Sir, eight annas for a bottle!"

Ghalib who was reposed comfortably in his chair, unconcerned with this small talk asked, "By when shall we get the money?"

"Within four or five days, and if God be willing, before Id, but this petition must bear your signature...without it perhaps..."

Haji put the papers before Ghalib, who shuffled through those twenty filled sheafs and asked, "Where shall I put my signature?"

Haji flipped over the pages to the last leaf simultaneously pulling out an inkpot and a pen from under the table. Mirza dipped the pen into the inkpot and scribbled his signature on the paper. Haji and Shams looked at each other from the corner of their smiling eyes.

Mirza got up, untied his horse and mounted it.

"I shall take your leave now, Shams?" He tugged at the reins of the house and spurred away.

4

Ghalib place a pillow for Umrao on the *palang* (bed) as she said, "A man doesn't grow up writing verses. Will you ever understand the affairs of the world?"

Ghalib tried to placate her anger with his smile. "Tell me then, what should have I done—brought the papers to you?"

"And that lawyer of yours—Hiralal—what is he for? You could have said that you need to show the papers to him and that you would sign them only on his advice..."

Ghalib sat down beside her and said, "Now...now, don't you frown so often, the kid will have frowns impressed on his forehead even before it is born."

"And you, you too can't stay without bothering me."

"You need not worry, dear. Next Thursday I shall go to Mehrauli and ask for the money. I'll ask for the papers if they do not give me the money."

"As if they would return the papers to you. Does anyone leave a bird held in their hand?"

"Their trust, they must account for, why shall I spoil mine—and that too for a fowl filtcher?"

Wafadar appeared at the door. Umrao beckoned her in.

"The masseuse has arrived..." Wafadar said.

"Call her in!" Begum said.

Mirza got up to leave.

"When is the baby expected?" he asked on his way to the doorway. Umrao smiled, "Grace be to the Lord! On the day of Id."

Mirza beamed with happiness. "Then Id shall call for double celebrations." He paused at the parrot cage, crooned affectionately to it and said, "Mitthu Miyan, you have neither kids nor family, why have you put on a long face?"

He left the room with this final flourish and hardly had he stepped out of the room that the masseuse entered.

5

"Allah knows when they will pass a verdict on the pension," Shams said as he pulled out two muslin bags that were tucked in his sash. He offered them to Ghalib and said, "Here is the money, Asad Bhai—450 in one and 300 in the other, 750 in all—and that's all we've got from the royal treasury for now." The sun fell brightly on Ghalib as he moved away from the shadow of the inn. He addressed Haji without looking back, "Haji, when are you going to Agra?"

"Tomorrow."

"Do me a favour then, give this 350 to my brother Yusuf. You know Yusuf Miyan, don't you? And ask him to write to me."

He turned to Shams and said, "I'll take your leave Shams, and I'm taking your horse, shall send it back from Meerut." He mounted the horse and galloped away.

"What work does he have in Meerut?"

"You get English wine at the cantonment. That's where he is heading now that he has got the money," Haji said.

"What! Will he spend all that money on wine?"

"Only god knows how much he spends on it!"

6

Ghalib entered the gate with a donkey load of whisky crates. He asked the owner to stop at the door, cautioning him to be careful, "There's wares of glass in the cargo, unload it diligently. I'll send for my man."

He stepped into the inner coutyard of the house and shouted for Kalloo. Wafadar appeared instead.

"Where's Kallo Miyan?" Ghalib enquired. "Ask him to take those crates off the donkey-back."

"What have you brought, *Huzoor-e-alla*?"

"Nothing that may interest you, and tell me, is Begum all by herself? Can I go in?"

"Please go in. Several times she has asked about you—whether you have come back from Mehrauli."

Ghalib entered the room. Umrao sat up on the bed. "Been out long. Where have you been?"

"Nowhere in particular—around the cantonment in Meerut," a smile knotted his face.

"Did you get the money from Shams?"

"Yes, 750—I asked Haji to reach one half to Yusuf Mirza."

Umrao caught her head in her hands.

"Now what wrong have I done?"

"Will Haji reach the money to him?" she almost screamed.

Mirza placed a hand on her tummy and playfully admonished, "Soften your tone dear, let not the baby hear you or else it may take you for a difficult mother."

"You," she instantly lowered her tone, "cross all limits. How could you trust Haji?"

"Dear, if he gave me the money, why shouldn't he reach the money to Yusuf," there was simplicity in his deduction.

"And what did you do with the remaining half?" she tried to be calm.

"Paid off the grocer."

"And the draper?"

"Him too."

"And the tiles?"

"Tiled it away."

She was about to react when Ghalib added smilingly, "Paid for it too, I did."

"And the rest?"

"Spent it on bottles of liquor."

"Why so?"

"Because the creator has only promised for the daily bread. He didn't provide for the drink — so I got it myself."

Umrao was visibly annoyed but kept her silence. Her eyes moistened with tears. "Begum," Ghalib tried to offer an explanation, "the friends are asking for a treat. I had promised to celebrate the arrival of the new born and Id. Now tell me, why would anyone come home for a dry dinner. Don't you want to celebrate the arrival of the newcomer?"

Umrao was somewhat pacified and asked softly, "What wrong would it have been to be in possession of a little money at Id?"

"More will come, dear. Lala is to come here a day before Id. He had taken my *diwan* to Lucknow for publication—he is to bring in some advance."

7

"So the Nawal Kishore people too refused to publish it?"

Ghalib's voice came over Bansidhar, who was sitting before a small table. A few pages were scattered on the table, and a folder housed the pages of his *diwan*. The two friends occasionally stole a look at the folder. It was evident that the folder held the comfort of a glory that had been unduly denied.

"Nobody was interested in publishing it, no one...I tried my best," Bansidhar found it difficult to assimilate the reality of the situation.

Ghalib sighed. He had been standing near a parapet, looking at the goings-on in his inner courtyard like a god who had his magical power taken away from him, a god impotent to do anything. From his vantage point, he watched a midwife cross the courtyard with a pot of hot water; Wafadar in an unusual hurry, clutching at a bundle of rags; Kalloo lighting up a fire for Wafadar to take in and at Wafadar again, walking across the courtyard, the rags in one hand, the pot of water in the other with smoke hovering over it. He thought of a couplet as he turned his attention to his friend in the room:

"Zindagi apni jab iss shakl mein guzri Ghalib
Hum bhi kya yaad karyenge ke Khuda rakhte the."

If this is the shape of thing in life, Ghalib
We'll remember that we had a God, who shaped them.

Ghalib had hardly sat down that a shriek leaped up from the room below, the pain of creation. His face broke into a smile. Another shriek leaped up in succession, higher than the one before, higher than the ceiling of the room, with the ease of death. He aged again. Ghalib run down the stairs in a tearing hurry with Bansidhar hot on his heels. He dashed across the courtyard and the midwife came to the door, sobbing. He looked at her, his face hurled questions at her.

"Begum," the midwife said between sobs, "is well by the grace of the lord." And she turned her face to the wall.

Ghalib slowly stepped forward and stood in front of her, catching sight of Wafadar, who sobbed incessantly against a pillar. Kalloo stood frozen at the head of the corridor, numb till his bones.

"And the child?" Ghalib stared at the midwife, tears beginning to cloud his eyes.

"Still born," the midwife somehow managed to bring herself together to say it.

A whole world drowned in a few drops of tears that betrayed Ghalib's feelings. He walked past Bansidhar who was standing in the courtyard. Ghalib reached for the stairs.

A strong gust of wind stealthily entered the terrace room, sneaked into the folder, and essayed to elope with the sheafs of poetry that had once driven their calligrapher crazy, and by the time Ghalib could reach his room, only a single leaf lay stuck to the folder. The rest was blown away into the street. He picked up the single sheaf: three couplets sat comfortably on the page:

"Dil hi tho hai na sang O khist, dard se bhar na aae kyun?
Ro'ainge hum hazar baar, koi humein satae kyun?

Qaid-e hayat O band-e gham, asl mein dono ek hain:
Maut se pehle admi gham se nijat pae kyun?

Ghalib-e-khastha ke baghair kuan se kaam band hain
Ro'aiey zar zar kya? kiji-e haaye haaye kyun?"

A heart after all, is not stone, why must not it brim with pain
A thousand tears shall I shed, why must people hurt me.

Ties of life are the ties of sorrow.
Before death, there is no respite from sorrow.

The world does not slow down for an embittered Ghalib
Why must the heart cry for it, why must a fuss be made about it.

He stood with his gaze fixed at the paper for an eternity and then let go of it. Another gust of wind picked it up in its embrace.

five

I

A FLAME FLICKERED, larger than life and busted. The smoke house, the *chandukhana*, was filled with smoke. Walls of smoke hid people from view. And even through these smoky curtains, a man sought to identify a fellow smoker as he entered the portals of the *chandukhana*.

"Fiddan!"

"Yes...Khursheed!"

"You have stepped in here after an age! You were not to be seen even at the last *mushaira* at Id?"

Fiddan found a *takia* (pillow) in a corner, crossed his legs and said, "I believe it was a wonderful evening and I'm made to understand that Ustad Zauq stole the show."

"Of course—what did you expect? He is the emperor's ustad for no other reason—did he recite a fine gazal that night."

"Aab to ghabra ke yeh kehte hain ke marjaenge
Mar gaey per na laga ji—to kidher jaenge"

In fear I now say I'd better die
But if peace be not in death, whither then?

Another acquaintance of theirs joined in their conversation, "He wasn't seen, that friend of ours from Agra?"

"Who—Mirza Ghalib?"

"Yes, him."

"Why would that pagan come to an Id *mushaira*? He too is a brother to Mir, and would be turned out of Delhi in a similar fashion," Khursheed said. "Haven't you heard that couplet by Mir:

"Mir ke din-O-mazhab ko ab pochhte kya ho, uss ne tho
Qashqa khaincha, der mein baitha, kab ka tark Islam kya!"

My faith and my religion,
I've pulled at pipes, sat at temples and argued erelong with Islam.

"He would engage in much futile talk," he paused to gauge the effect his words had on his listeners and then added, "I had heard that Mirza celebrated Diwali with grandeur, but dressed his house in mourning at Id."

"Lord, O Lord, faith and piety are being eroded from this earth of ours. Chhenu, pass me the *chillum*, I'll take a drag in the name of the Lord—woe betide such pagans—where all do they come from to settle in Dilli!" Fiddan hid behind a cloud of marijuana smoke.

2

Mirza stared at the half-burnt candle, a dozen letters yet to be posted scattered around and their envelopes stacked together. Outside, the night reposed in pitch darkness. Mirza looked from the candle to the melting wax to the paper spread in front of him. He clutched a pen in one hand. The silence of the night was punctuated with shrill cries of the night watchman, cries that pushed the curtains of Mirza's windows to let him know that another denizen of the night was up, out on the roads. The events of the day were hard for Ghalib to chase from his mind. However hard he tried to erase them from his memory, all the more difficult it would become: the grave of his little one and that petite red flower that had a smear of black on it. That flower seemed to have talked to him when he kneeled down to offer his prayers at the grave, it seemed as if his own child had sprung up from the bowels of the earth and yet...

He dipped the pen in the inkpot and wrote:

Sab kahan, kuch lala-O-gul mein numayan ho gaien
Khak mein kya surtein hongi ke pinhan ho gaien!

Not everything, a few were displayed in that red flower
The earth hid some marvellous faces in her bowels.

He cast a glance at the bottle on the edge of the table and the empty glass. The bottle had a little whisky still in it.

Ranj se khugar hua insaan tho mit jata hai ranj
Mushkilain mujh par parein itni ke asaan ho gaien.

Accustomed to sorrow if a man becomes, then sorrow too loses its sting
Difficulties fell so many upon me that it became easy to grapple with.

Yo'n hi gar rota raha Ghalib, to aye ehl-e jahan
Dekhna in bastiyon ko tum, ke veeran hogaien.

And if this be the way of the world, then O you men of the world
You would then witness the ruin of this civilization.

The night continued its song of silence.

3

The song of the blind fakir singing once again pierced the lane of Gali Qasim. "*Mayie,*" he came to the doorsteps and asked for the lady of the house. Umrao looked up from the breakfast tray that she was helping Kalloo fix for her husband, and enquired of Wafadar, "Is it Tuesday today?"

"Yes, *Bibiji,*" Wafadar confirmed.

"This Brahmin comes every Tuesday. Go! Give him a bowl of flour."

Wafadar scooped a bowl of flour from the container and went out of the doorway.

Holding the breakfast tray, Kalloo who had left with the breakfast tray, crossed the courtyard and went up the stairs. He peeped in through the half open door and sought permission to enter. He waited for an answer, in the absence of which he entered the room and not finding Mirza there placed the tray on the table and came out on the terrace. He called for Begum from the terrace, "Bibi Sahiba, *Huzoor-alla* is not in his room."

Umrao came out to the verandah.

"Allah! He is out without his breakfast once again," she sighed.

"He seems to be worried since a few days," Kalloo adding in his bit of concern.

"That's but obvious. Since the death of his child he seems to keep aloof, even from me. Allah knows the reason of his annoyance with me."

"Why should he be annoyed with you? He is worried, that's why he sits at Haji Mir's shop from the morning, burying himself in loads of books and thus whiling his day away," Kalloo consoled Umrao.

4

Ghalib sat surrounded with piles of books, leafing through an old anthology of Mir. Haji Mir was engaged in dusting the racks of books. Two British soldiers crossed the shop on horseback. Mirza shut the book that he was reading and stared vacantly at the patch of street illuminated with bright sunlight. Mir caught him thus. He casually asked without exhibiting unnecessary interest in his friend's affairs, "I have noticed that you are worrying a great deal these days. Keep hope, He is there, some way or the other, things will work out."

"Koi umeed bar nahin aati
Koi soorat nazar nahin aati."

No hope comes true
No sight of it comes near.

Ghalib commented as he rubbed his eyes to keep them from shutting due to sleeplessness.

"You haven't slept last night, have you?" Haji Mir enquired.

"Maut ka ek din mu'iayn hai
Neend kyun raat bhar nahin aati."

Death will come in the end
Why does sleep elude the night.

Mir nodded smilingly, in admiration,

"Smells fresh, note it down. I'll keep it safely, god knows how many of your creations have gone unnoted!" He extended a piece of paper towards him.

"Mir Saheb," Ghalib said as he wrote it down, "I think I shall better be off to Lucknow—in the court of Nawab Asif-ud-Daullah I may find a place."

"Mirza, don't you be under this impression. There's great rivalry between Dilli and Lucknow. The Lucknowwallahs don't let the Dilliwallahs read their poems in their city..."

"But I'm not even a Diliwallah," Mirza said.

"It's true that you are from Agra but..." Mir tried to argue.

"Not even from Agra, Mir Saheb!

"Hoon garia-e nishat-e tassawar se naghma zan,
Mein undelib-e gulshan na aafrida hoon."

I'm the nightingle from the garden that has not yet been created.

Mir took the paper on which Mirza had noted down his couplets.

"Will that garden be ever created?" he enquired.

Mirza got up with ease and said casually, "Yes, Mir Saheb, when a single Hindustan is born out of the womb of Dilli, Lucknow, Agra, Hyderabad, in that garden I am bound to find a place for myself. Mir Saheb, I'm a poet of Urdu—not of a city and Urdu is the language of this whole country, of the entire people of this country, not of the fort, or of the nawabs or of the king emperors."

A silence ensued for a while. Mirza put on his shoes that had been left at the threshold. And then, all of a sudden, a breeze wafted in the broken lyrics of a ghazal that a feminine voice had lent more credulence to:

"Dil hi tho hai na sang-O-khist, dard se bhar na aae kyun?"

A heart after all is not stone, why must not it brim with pain...?

Ghalib craned his neck to trace the voice. He looked meaningfully at Mir who said, "It's your verse Mirza, isn't it?"

"Yes," Ghalib made no efforts to mask his surprise, "and it is for the first time in Dilli, that lips that are not mine have pronounced my verses."

The next couplet came on the wings of the wind.

"How did your ghazal reach the courtesan?" there was wonder in Mir's enquiry.

"Yes, that fascinates me too," Ghalib said, "who could fling an earthly thing at the heavens?"

5

"Der nahin — haram nahin — dar nahin — aastan nahin
Baithe hain reh - guzar pe hum ..."

The voice stopped midway.

The ghazal came in drafts and Ghalib crossed the road to climb the stairs of the courtesan's house, the *kotha*.

Through the silky, translucent curtains of a half-opened door, Ghalib saw a young girl singing the ghazal. Her eyes caught sight of the intruder at the door and she stopped abruptly.

"Who are you?" she asked, her kohl-lined eyes repeated the question with sincere intensity.

"Pardon me," Ghalib said, "but the ghazal dragged me here."

"Do you know whose verses these are?" she asked as she came to the door, though still behind the silky veil of the curtain.

"Yes, my friend's, Mirza Ghalib's. It is a fragment of his ghazal. Where did you get it from?"

"A grocer had wrapped some powder in it," she laughed lightly. "One couplet was erased, the other was torn away—I only got a unfinished verse in the bargain." She showed him the wrapper.

Ghalib looked at the crumpled piece of paper and recited:

"Haan woh nahin Khuda parast, jao woh be-wafa sahi
Jis ko ho din-O-dil aziz, uss ki gali mein jae kyun!"

Count not, amongst the faithful, let him be an unloyalist
Why must a lover of faith and religion go to his lane.

She lingered over the couplet and then hurriedly turned to her paper and pen, "If you may permit me, I'll note it down."

Ghalib recited the couplet once again.

"Hai Allah! Wah!" she was ecstatic.

Ghalib recited the concluding couplet,

"Ghalib-e khastha ke baghair kaun se kaam band hain..."

The world does not slow down for an embittered Ghalib...

"Ghalib-e khastha ke baghair kaun se kaam band hain,"
she ruminated over the verse, transported to another world.

"Ro'aiey zar zar kyaa? kiji-e haaye haaye kyun?"

Why must the heart cry for it, why must a fuss be made about it.

Ghalib completed the couplet as if that was his final flourish on the stage and bowed out.

The courtesan called out after him, "Tell me...tell me, who is this Ghalib?"

He was at the head of the stairs and did not turn back.

"Poochhte hain woh ke Ghalib kaun hai!
koi batlao ke hum batlaeen kya?"

She asks me who is this Ghalib,
May be someone needs to tell me what to say.

Ghalib said to himself as he climbed down the stairs.

6

Ghalib returned to Mir Saheb's shop and sat down on the stool.

"Did you meet her?" Mir enquired.

Ghalib smiled.

"Mir Saheb," he asked after a brief lapse of time, "verses that are sung by both, a faqir and a courtesan do not perish, or do they?"

The sound of the ghazal from the courtesan's house above the shop once again wrapped the friends in its embrace. Both turned to look up.

7

On the stairs that led to the courtesan's house sat a bulky, lovelorn Pathan, and the voice of the courtesan's maid could be faintly heard in complaint to her employer, "That Pathan is still sitting on the stairs."

"Let him," said Nawabjaan, the courtesan and brushed aside the complaint.

The maid's next complaint was not audibly pronounced, "Oh, not again this ghazal of Ghalib, she has sung it ten times since the morning."

Unmindful of her maid's opinion, Nawab began to sing the ghazal once again. Slowly at first, then at full cresendo. Her voice seemed to come from deep within her, filling her body, her soul, echoing softly in the room, gingerly fondling the lacy curtains, flowing on silk outside the confines of her room, onto the street, reverberating in the air:

"Dil hi tho hai na sang-O- khist, dard se bhar na aae kyun?
Ro'aingay hum hazaar baar, koi humein sataae kyun?

Der nahin haram nahin, dar nahin aastan nahin
Baithe hain rehguzer pe hum, ghair humein uthai kyun?

Haan woh nahin Khuda parast, jao woh be wafa sahi
Jis ko ho din-O-dil aziz, uss ki gali mein jae kyun!

Ghalib-e khastha ke baghair kaun se kaam band hain
Ro'aiey zar zar kyaa? kiji-e haaye haaye kyun?"

A heart after all, is not stone, why must not it brim with pain,
A thousand tears shall I shed, why must people hurt me?

Not in a temple, not at Kaaba, nor at a door, not even the threshold,
I'm out on the road, why must people remove me?

Count not him amongst the faithful, let him be an unloyalist,
Why must a lover of faith and religion go to his lane?

The world does not slow for an embittered Ghalib,
Why must the heart cry for it, why must a fuss be made about it?

six

I

THE STREET REVERBERATED with life under a clear blue sky. Shops lined the street and their canopies fluttered in the cool autumn breeze.

A motley crowd stood in a circle marking an arena in which two cocks were engaged in a deadly combat. An excitement ran through the crowd, interrupted with shrieks of jubilation that reflected their merriment.

A man rode a brown, brawny horse with an authoritative gallop onto the street. A man bound in ropes tagged along.

"The Kotwal!" someone exclaimed. The man on the mount spurred the horse.

"Run for your lives, brother!" another shrieked. And in a moment, the motley surge of crowd had broken into a dash of colour on one shop, a tinge of blue at the other. Even the cocks seemed to have received the full import of the words and had let go their hold on one another and occupied themselves better. The man tugged at his reins and the horse neighed to a halt.

"Who engaged them in fight?" he nearly barked. The horse bucked, and the Kotwal's moustaches twitched in anger. The cocks looked up innocently at the man.

"The hens," somebody decided to be wise.

"They themselves were fighting, Kotwal Saheb, take them to prison." The cocks wobbled away.

"My name's not Munir Khan if I do not expunge this habit of gambling from this city of Dilli." He went red to his roots.

An old man pointed towards the man bound in ropes and asked, "Why have you caught Rashid Ali, Kotwal Saheb? What for?"

"The same thing that you were doing the other day—gambling! And warn that noble poet of yours, someday I'll catch him red-handed at his game. That Mirza ridicules me a lot." He galloped away with this warning, his prisoner in tow.

2

Umrao found Ghalib slouched on the *diwan*, his eyes shut, as she entered the living room. He had her *dupatta* wrapped around his hand. She approached him stealthily and tried to remove the dupatta. He opened his eyes.

"So, you are awake?" she was taken aback, "and why have you tied my duppatta in knots?"

"They are verses, Begum," Ghalib said, "I tie them to your dupatta but the knots fall somewhere else."

"Is there someone? Has your heart been in knots?" she laughingly complained.

He smiled and nodded his head.

"If there's someone, bring her home..."

"The shackle of one leg has ushered me in difficulties, if I wear another one, it would be really difficult to walk then."

She sat down on the *diwan* and said, "I have been noticing your increasing aloofness from me for quite some time. Who is the reason for this growing distance between us?"

"Don't you know what occupies me from morning to eve?"

"Sau pusht se hai peshae aaba sepahgeri
Kuch shayri zariya-e izzat nahin mujhe."

She got up and stood beside him, resting her head against the bedpost, "But people say that you are carefree—the way you drink and gamble makes people believe that you have no worry."

"What does the world know about the reason for my drinking or why I gamble? If I do not indulge in these activities I'll suffocate to death. Just because I laugh away my sorrows, they think I do not know how to cry."

"But I've never seen you cry," she said teasingly.

"Un ke dekhe se jo aajati hai mounh per rounaq
Woh samajhte hain ke bimar ka haal achha hai."

A sheen appears on my face when I see her
She gets the impression that I'm no longer ailing.

Ghalib's smile was silhouetted against the call of the *azaan*.

"*Allah*! Time for my *namaz*." Begum exclaimed picking up the Jaae-Namaaz. But before she could move away, Ghalib gathered her in his arms and said, "So you wanted to know who pulls us apart—you've heard him now."

She touched her ears as if atoning for her husband's seemingly blasphemous act, "*Tauba! Tauba!* What sacrilegious talk you indulge in."

"Achcha Begum! You read the *namaz* five times a day, is there so much to say to *Allah Miyan*?" Ghalib laughed lightly.

"What's in it for you—you neither fast nor pray."

"You're right, dear, but you'll marvel at my sight on the Day of Judgement. You will be with those men in a blue loin cloth, a rosary in one hand and a *lota* for *wuzoo* in the other, and I in the group of king emperors like Namrud, Firaun who may have sinned but..."

"*Tauba! Tauba!* Oh, the merciful one! Have mercy on him, forgive him," she touched her ears once again and ran out of the room to kneel at the call of the lord.

As she left, Kalloo came to the door and from behind the curtain said, "*Huzoor-e-wala*, somebody has come to meet you."

"Who's it?" Ghalib asked.

"I haven't seen him before."

"Ask him to wait."

Kalloo left and Ghalib got up to give an audience to his visitor.

He came out of the room and found Begum kneeling in prayer in the courtyard. He picked up his tender calf skin shoes and tiptoed across the courtyard muttering, "Converted the whole courtyard into a veritable prayer house, into an entire masjid, and if one has to cross the well shod, woe betide."

3

He came out to his doorstep to find Fiddan waiting for him, who raised his hand in greeting at the very sight of Ghalib. There was a puzzlement in his eyes as he searched his memory to place the man.

"Ghalib's your name, Sir?" the man asked.

"Yes, my nom-de-plume. What business brings you here?"

Ghalib's memory was a complete blank.

"My mistress has sent a message for you, Sir," Fiddan handed over a rolled letter to Ghalib. His head was bowed in attendance.

Ghalib, still unable to unravel the mystery of the message, unrolled the letter: "I had chanced upon the fragments of a ghazal of yours...and a gentleman came over on hearing me sing it and joined the fragments into one. Said he was a friend of yours and if you send me another of your ghazals, I shall be indebted to you for life." The letter was signed—a humble admirer of Ghalib.

A smile stretched Ghalib's lips and a pride burnished bright on his face.

"How are you engaged there?" Ghalib asked the messenger.

"An attendant, Sir," Fiddan said.

"Where did you find my address?"

"There's a bookseller right in front of our stairs—one Mir Saheb, I got your address from him, Sir," Fiddan said, satisfying Ghalib's curiosity.

Ghalib asked Fiddan to follow him and as he turned towards the stairs, the verses of a new ghazal dawned on him:

"Dil-e nadan tujhe hua kya hai?
Aakhir iss dard ki dawa kya hai

Hum ko un se wafa ki hai umeed
Jo nahin jante wafa kya hai."

Oh you innocent heart, what's become of you,
What is the way out of this pain?

I long for loyalty from the one
Who knows not what loyalty is.

4

The city Kotwal entered the living room of Nawabjaan's *kotha* as she brought to life Ghalib's new ghazal. He was dressed in the finery of the evening, a delicate chain of white fragrant flowers carelessly wrapped around his wrist. He took his seat as Nawabjaan sang.

"Dil-e nadan tujhe hua kya hai?
Aakhir iss dard ki dawa kya hai

Hum hain mushtaq aur woh bezar
Ya ilahi ye majra kya hai?"

Oh you innocent heart what's become of you,
What is the way out of this pain?

I am so eager and he so disinterested,
Oh lord, what is this affair?

The few people who sat in audience their mouths filled with beetle juice, applauded. Nawabjaan acknowledged their salutations and sang further:

"Jab ke tujh bin nahin koi moujood
Phir ye hangama aye Khuda kya hai?

When there is no one present but you,
What's this brouhaha all about?

Jaan tum par nisar karta hoon
Main nahin janta dua kya hai."

She stole a glance at her mother, who sat next to her. She smiled, exhibiting her paan-stained teeth as Nawabjaan wove magic into the last couplet:

"Jaan tum par nisar karta hoon
Main nahin ..."

I bestow my life on you, know not I...

5

The sound of Ghalib's footsteps on the stairs broke the silence of the night. He crossed the courtyard and entered Umrao's room, who sat on the *dastarkhwan*, a low height dining chair, eating.

"When did you return?" she asked as soon as she spotted him.

"Where from?" Ghalib was puzzled.

"How do I know where you go?" she said.

A faint whiff of alcohol invaded her nostrils as Ghalib tried to answer her complaint. She covered her nose politely, even as Ghalib spoke, "Haven't been out since the morning, dear, not even for a moment."

He reached out to grab a morsel from her plate, but she pulled the plate away. It tugged at his heart and reflected on his face.

"Kalyan," she called for the servant, "please get a dinner plate and glass for Saheb."

"Have you separated my utensils, dear?" Ghalib tried hard to translate the emotion on his face into one of humour.

"No, not yours, I've segregated mine—do not mind it. I fear for my faith."

The mask of joviality slipped from his face. Beneath it, he was raw, hurt and wounded. He put himself together, endeavoured to dab his face in humour once again and said, "Only he need to fear who has something to lose—you have faith, that's why you are scared, and I," He pointed his finger towards her, "have nothing but this faithful of mine."

"Why are you so disenchanted with God?"

"Forbear dear, not disenchanted with the Lord, not with him—the only difference is that I do not crawl and beg and plead before Him like the rest. Have you seen kids ever crawl and beg favour from their parents the way you do with the Almighty?" he paused and then added, "my relations with God are more informal than yours."

"Is that why he never listens to you?"

"Perhaps He too does not understand my verses!" he chuckled.

"*Astghafirullah!*" she said as she got up, "O Lord, forgive him for his pride." And she walked out of the room.

6

Mir Saheb sat in his shop briming with books sheafing through loose leaves of Ghalib's poems.

"*Adaab!*" a beautiful young voice broke into his privacy.

Mir Saheb looked up from the poems. A woman in a veil partially screened the doorway.

"Yes, madam?" Mir Saheb said.

"There's a poet by the name of Ghalib—I am not familiar with his full name—do you have an anthology of his poetry?" she unveiled an eagerness as she asked Mir.

"Not yet published," Mir smiled, "but, yes, I do possess a few ghazals, a few verses of his, he writes them down whenever he happens to grace the shop with his presence."

"Does Ghalib come here?" an excitement surrogated her earlier eagerness.

"Yes, he does," he showed her the loose papers in his hand, "these are in his very writing."

She would have snatched the pages from his hand but decency forbade it. She took the pages, glanced over them and read a couplet aloud:

"Pehle aati thi haale dil pe hansi
Ab kisi baat par nahin aati."

I used to laugh at the state of my heart earlier
But not a thing humours me now.

An excitement surged down her spine. She stood enchanted, at a moment laughing at the state of her heart, at another quiet, calm.

"But where did you learn about him?" Mir asked enthusiastically.

"Will you let me keep these verses of his?" she said, oblivious of the question she had been asked.

"I need to ask him," he said apologetically, "nobody has asked for his verses before." He caught sight of Ghalib who had just come and stood behind her, and said, "Lo, he is here."

She turned and lifted her veil. They faced each other and she gasped.

"You!" her eyes were wide with wonder, "you had come over the other day!"

"Yes, I, the perpetrator of that imprudence," Ghalib bowed in reply.

There was an awkward moment and then she said, "And silly me, I didn't even ask you in, sent you off from the door." There was a hint of regret in her voice.

"Main gaya waqt nahin hoon ke phir kabhi na aa sakun."

Unlike the time passed by, I may be able to come again.

Ghalib smiled.

"May I keep these verses with me?" she asked, almost pleadingly, showing him the loose sheafs.

"Please," Ghalib waved casually:

"Naghma ho jata hai waan, gar nala mera jaye hai."

Only a song would blossom if my heartburn reaches there.

She bowed, touched her forehead with her hand and with the same fever of excitement expressed her gratitude as she left abruptly. She suddenly stopped, as if pulled by a remembrance, turned and thanked Mir Saheb. A richness almost immediately set into her as she crossed over to climb the stairs to her house.

Mir Saheb turned to Ghalib, "Did you notice how fast the colour faded off her face?"

Ghalib recited:

"Ho ke aashiq, woh pari rukh aur nazuk ban gaya
Rang khulta jaye hai, jitna ke urtha jaye hai."

In love, the angel-faced became all the more tender
Her colour, the faster, the more it fades.

"That's your verse too, Mirza Nausha," Mir Saheb said at last as he sat down,

"Ishq par zor nahin, hai ye woh aatish, Ghalib,
Jo lagae na lage aur bujhae na bane."

There's no rein on love, it's that fire Ghalib,
That you can't either light or blow out at will.

Ghalib heaved a sigh, deposited his load of books at Mir Saheb's counter, "I had come to return your books, Mir Saheb, I beg your leave now."

"Where to?" Mir Saheb was surprised, "you've hardly just come...now where are you off to?"

"To the residence of Mathura Das—to seek a loan..."

Mir Saheb looked up. Ghalib added, "I sent some money for my younger brother through Khwaja Haji, but he disappeared. The money didn't reach my brother—and a message from him read the expenses on his treatment..." Mirza paused a while.

"Woe betide the ill-wisher of Mirza Yusuf, but is he ill?" Mir filled in the pause.

"Yes. Knocked off at the head. Saved from the feelings of pain—has three children and a wife for me to care. If I call it a burden, I'm guilty of a crime and you know my income." A sadness escaped Mirza and Mir Saheb too felt it. He looked at Ghalib through sad, emotionless eyes as he took his leave.

"God be with you Mirza, *Khuda Hafiz!*" his lips tremored as he bid adieu to Mirza.

7

Ghalib had hardly walked a little distance when a voice from behind besieged him to stop.

Fiddan greeted Ghalib as he turned to trace the caller.

"Nawabjaan has sent me to ask you the meaning of a verse..."

"A beautiful name she has," Ghalib started, "yes?" he goaded Fiddan who read out a verse in difficult Urdu.

"Waa'n woh ghurur anz-O-naaz
Yaa'n ye hejaab-e paas-e waze."

He waited for a moment and then commented,

"A very uncommon turn of phrase you do have, Sir!"

"Rah mein hum milen kahan
Bazm mein woh bulaye kyun."

"Tell her," Ghalib replied, " 'where do I meet her in
the way, why must she invite me to her hearth.' "

"Thank you, Sir!" Fiddan bowed and turned back repeating the line over and over again, "Rah mein hum milen kahan, Bazm..."

Ghalib watched him and smiled.

"Qaasid ke aate aate khat ik aur likh rakhun
Main janta hoon woh jo likhenge jawab mein."

I shall write another letter before her messenger comes.
For I know what her reply will be.

Ghalib stood on a raised plinth in the garden thinking about the couplets of the ghazal.

8

His face broke into a smile.

"Kab se hoon kya batao'n, jahan-e kharaab mein
Shabhae hijr ko bhi rakhun gar hisaab mein

Mujh tak kab un ki bazm mein aata tha daur-e jaam
Saqi ne kuchh mila na dia ho sharaab mein

Ta phir na intezar mein, neend aae umer bhar
Aane ka wada kar gae, aae jo khuwaab mein

Ghalib chuti sharaab par, ab bhi kbhi kbhi
Pita hoon roz-e abr-O-shab-e mahtaab mein."

Know not since when am I under this cast of misfortune
Not even if I keep an account of the nights of parting.

Never in her gathering did the wine goblet find its way to me,
The winemaid might have adulterated the wine.

In waiting for her, sleep eluded me for a life time.
Though she had promised to come once when she had come in my dreams,

And though I had foresworn drinking
Yet, at times I do on cloudy days and moonlit nights.

seven

I

A CRACKER SPAT fire and the horse neighed and lifted its forelegs. Its mount, a British soldier, almost lost grasp of the reins. His eyes scanned the entire market square. The motley surge of people, unperturbed, carried on with their activities. The soldier, splendid in his livery, crackled in short spats of fire.

"Who is that bastard?" he clutched desperately at the reins.

Another burst of cracker startled the horse.

"You bloody fool! Stop it...you fool...I'll kill you...come out!"

A hush fell around the market place. The silence irked the soldier. He lost his temper and shouted, "*Koun hai?* You son of a bitch...come out...dirty blackies...I'll see you!"

He jerked his head up in anger. People stood in their balconies, at their windows; even Ustad Zauq stood in his balcony, a mute witness to the act.

Another cracker went off but this time nobody spoke, nobody moved from their places. People sat in their shops, on the stairs of the masjid and remained where they were. A silence stood well pronounced in the market square, carefully punctuated with a burst of crackers from all directions. One after the other. In seasoned successions. The horse neighed again. The soldier's grasp on the reins loosened. Beads of cold perspiration outlined his eyebrows.

Ustad Zauq pulled together the curtains on the balcony and glided into the room where a few poets sat surrounding a makeshift fire. Zauq took his seat to a fading applause. He said, rubbing the palms of his hands together, "Encore, Momin Miyan! Encore, I didn't hear the verses. Excuse me, encore please."

"Tum mere paas hote ho goya
Jab koi doosra nahin hota."

You are with me
When nobody is with me.

"*Wah, wah, subhanallah,*" gushed an appreciative audience.
Momin Miyan recited his couplets to waves of applause.

"Haal dil yaar ko likhoon kyun kar
Hath dil se juda nahin hota,"

How do I write to my friend the state of my heart,
The hand parts not from the heart,

"Chaar-e dil siwae sabra nahin
So tumhare siwa nahin hota."

Zauq savoured one of his couplets and then added, "May I be permitted to read out one of my fresh verses..."

"*Irshaad,*" the gathering said in one voice giving him the go-ahead.

Zauq was about to recite his verse, when the sound of a cracker bursting outside disturbed him.

"What's going on outside?" Momin asked.

"A burst of a cracker, I believe," someone answered.

"Yes, I believe so. Had it been shots of gunfire, you would have heard accompanying screams."

"Nothing to worry about," Zauq tried to assuage the gathering. "A discoloured Brit soldier is out in the lane caught in vollies of crackers by the people—two Brits together would have scared the city out of its wits..."

"Not cities alone, Sir…not anymore…now the entire nation is scared…"

"There is a hatred that seems to be brewing amongst the people," Zauq commented.

"You recite your verses, Sir," Shefta interrupted. "This is an everyday story and god knows when we shall get to hear your verses again."

Zauq once again sought the permission of the gathering to recite his verses and read,

"Laie hayat aae qaza le chali chale
Apni khushi na aae, na apni khushi chale,

Behter tho hai yahi ke na dunya se dil lage
Par kya karen jo kaam na be-dil-lagi chale,

Kam honge iss bisat par hum jaise badqumar
Jo chal hum chale so nehayat buri chale."

Life brought me here, let death take me away
I didn't come at will, it's not my will to go.

It's better that I do not get enchanted by this world
But I can't get around without being enchanted.

There would be few like us on this board
False are the moves that we make.

"And the concluding couplet is..." People cajoled him further and Zauq capped his ghazal to a round of applause.

"Jate hawaye shauq mein hain iss chaman se Zauq
Apni bala se bade saba ab kabhi chale."

2

The dice fell once again in Mirza's favour and the people at Sadiq's *chabutra* congratulated him.

"Wonderful, Mirza!" one said. "You do know how to do that really well."

"There is magic in your fingers," another towed the line.

And Sadiq said, "It's a losing affair to gamble with you, Mirza Nausha!"

And almost instantly, a man who had earlier informed Ghalib of the arrival of the Kotwal, announced the arrival of another guest.

Ghalib looked at his visitor, "Come over, Miyan, what's the name gentle folks call you by?"

"This humble servant is known by the name of Fiddan, Sir," the visitor said.

"Fiddan," Ghalib addressed his visitor by his name for the first time, "what brings you here?"

"I had gone to your residence, Sir," Fiddan said, "I learnt you that would be here—there is a message for you from Nawabjaan."

Ghalib read the message: "There is a mehfil (gathering) at my place tomorrow night. Let me have the honour to welcome you in my hearth and home. I want to sing your ghazal in your very presence. For God's sake, let not disappointment fall to my lot. Your blessed presence will liven the fate of my house and perhaps provide reason for someone to live. Yours Nawabjaan."

Ghalib sighed as he folded the letter and tucked it in his sash.

"Tell her that my wings are clipped before I can take flight. There are fetters on my feet and though incarceration is not dear to anyone, I am now imprisoned in the very habit of prison."

"Will you come then, Sir?" Fiddan asked.

Ghalib breathed in a pause and said, "I do not promise," then added with a wave of his hand. "Maybe I will."

Fidden saluted and retreated.

"Who's he?" Sadiq asked, "whose message did he bring?"

Ghalib puffed his plumes, craned his neck, and with an air of superiority answered with a swing in his tone, "We Mughals are strange, we take life out of those whom we die for/ I've taken the life out of one such *domini.*" He scooped the dice into his left hand and threw them on the board.

3

Nawabjaan stood tall against the mirror, giving final touches to her evening attire. She inched on her toes, looked once again at her reflection in the mirror and sat on the cot, her feet dangling on the side. The bright afternoon light defined every nook and corner of the room. Her maid squatted on the ground applying *alta* on her feet.

"What's the matter?" Malka, her mother looked at Nawabjaan. "For whom are you taking such pains to dress up? The evening is still a long way off."

"Amma," Nawabjaan pleaded, "Amma, would you braid my plait today, please?" she pleaded.

"Who is coming this evening?" Malka asked.

"The same, whose ghazal I shall sing, Mirza Ghalib."

"Will Mirza Ghalib grace our humble abode?" Malka asked.

Nawabjaan nodded her head in confidence,

"Uss pe ban jae kuch aisi ke bin aae na bane."

May something come upon him that there's no way but to come here.

She reached for her mother's hands, took them into hers, and said softly, "Amma, somebody has rightly said, these diaurnal balls of fire and cool are not sun and moon, for they come every day. Ghalib's status is beyond the reach of these suns and moons."

4

Ghalib pulled at his cloak, put on his *topi* and got ready to step out for the evening. His wife entered the room and seeing him in his old cloak said, "Take off this old one, I got a new one stitched for you—wear this one."

She helped him put on his new cloak.

"Begum," Ghalib said, "why do you dress me like a bridegroom? Would you care to know where I am headed for—to a *domini's* kotha and I have heard that she would give her life for me."

"And why shouldn't she," Begum replied with a smile. "The culmination of my dreams is no ordinary man."

"Is that so?" Ghalib asked. "And what may be the reason for your kindness towards me this evening?"

"Is it all right?" she asked, her hands around his neck as she tried to check the collar of the cloak. Ghalib's eyes fell on her bare arms that sported just two glass bangles.

An image of the past flashed through his mind.

5

Young Asad found it difficult to take his eyes off the glitter of the jewels around Umrao's neck and arms as she sat propped next to him on the *tonga*. The *tonga* jolted forward and she tapped on his shoulder with her closed fist. He looked at her with the familiarity of an old companionship at her bejewelled arms. She opened her fist which held a few coloured marbles. She passed them to him. He smiled as he took them in his hand and began to count them. The smile seemed to reach her lips too. He shifted his glance from the marbles, to her wrists adorned with gold bangles and then at the glitter of the necklace around her neck.

6

Ghalib's eyes rested on Umrao's slender, graceful neck, now bare. Two small gold studs in her ears stood like relics of a glorious past. She smiled as she checked the cloak for his comfort.

"You're very quiet today," she said. His eyes suddenly moistened, but he remained quiet and thoughtful, forcing her to ask, "You haven't anything to say. What is the matter?"

"Hai kuch aesi hi baat jo chup hoon
Warna kya baat kar nahin aati."

There must be something that quietens me
Otherwise I do have things to say.

"It's useless to talk to you," Umrao commented. "You resort to verses at the slightest excuse."

Quietness still pursed his lips together.

"I had asked you something. What thoughts are you lost in?"

"Hum wahan hain jahan se hum ko bhi
Kuchh humari khaber nahin aati."

I am there from where I too do not know what befalls me.

Saying this, Mirza walked off leaving Begum looking at his receding figure.

7

Lights illuminated Nawabjaan's house. A maid came in with a lamp and placed it in the room. Nawabjaan turned away from the blinds of the window, and away from the sights of the street. The maid looked at Nawabjaan, who looked quite pale.

"What disenchants you so acutely, madam?" she inquired.

"Nothing!" Nawabjaan said. "He must be about to come. Have you lit a lamp in the living room?"

"Yes, ma'am, Khan Saheb too has arrived."

The sounds of a sarangi being tuned accompanied with the sounds of the tabla sallied into Nawabjaan's room in a discordance of harmony. She peeped through the curtains into the hall and saw the Kotwal taking his seat.

"Where's Nawabjaan?" he enquired. "Hasn't she graced the *mehfil* as yet?" Nawabjaan dropped the curtain, her face livid with rage. "Gulrez," she addressed the maid, "have Mirza's cushion placed to the right."

"Yes ma'am," Gulrez bowed in obeisance.

8

Mirza sat at Sukhchain's counter lost in himself. The clinking of the gold coins knocked intermittently on his pensiveness. Sukhchain stacked the coins together and handed them over to Ghalib who almost immediately signed the pronote that Sukhchain had held out for him.

"And what made you want all this money so suddenly, Mirza Saheb? Are you out on a tour?" There was no chink in Mirza's armour of silence. He quietly pushed the signed pronote in his hand and sought permission to leave.

"Khuda Hafiz."

"God be with you, Mirza," the money lender prayed, more to God than Mirza and this he did gratis.

9

Nawabjaan entered the living room, and took her place in the center. Her guests were spread in a circle hemming the room, propped up against long upholstered cushions. A seat to Nawabjaan's right lay vacant awaiting the arrival of its guest. Nawabjaan took a long *alaap*. The sarangi player struck its cords to provide accompaniment to the lonesome *alaap*. She glided on with her *alaap*, stretching out the palm of her left hand in demonstration of an emotion, a *bhav*. Her hennaed palm told a story, a tale about to be unfolded. The Kotwal, smug in his evening liveries craned his neck to catch the changing moods of his beloved. There was a name calligraphed in henna on her palms and his curiosity got the better of him. His surprise knew no bounds when he took her hand in his, ostensibly in politeness, and tried to decipher it.

"Mirza!...Mirza who?"

Nawabjaan joined her palms and the Kotwal read aloud, "Mirza Ghalib! A bankrupt you've fallen in love with," he joked, "indebted to the entire age."

"And his debt that's accruing on the entire era! What about it? Generations after generations of Dilliwallahs will toil hard to repay it and...shall still fail," Nawabjaan replied in all seriousness.

"Oh ho!" the Kotwal reacted, "What do you know about him—whenever I chance to cross the streets of Ballimaran, I find him squatted deep in gambling. Someday he will be caught by me and then you would neither belong to him nor to his heart."

"Haan woh nahin Khuda parast, jao woh be wafa sahi
Jis ko ho din-O-dil aziz, uss ki gali mein jae kyun?"

Count not him amongst the faithful, let him be an unloyalist
Why must the one who holds faith and religion dear go to his lane,

Nawabjaan recited with a faint smile on her lips.

IO

Ghalib tapped Umrao Begum and as she turned, he dropped the gold ornaments into her lap.

"Wear them! Adorn your neck and your wrists."

She looked up and stared hard at him. Her face gave away myriad emotions—admiration, love and annoyance."Borrowed again?" she softly intoned.

Mirza nodded his head in affirmation.

"From whom?"

"Mathura Das doesn't give a single *cowrie,* not anymore. So I got it from Seth Sukhchain."

"But what was the need of all these?"

"Now, now, take off those glass bangles," he tried to gingerly pull at the bangles, "and wear these gold ones."

II

Lonesome, Nawabjaan's *alaap* was drawn into the vacant seat to her right like water currents in a whirlpool. Her *alaap* deepened, refuting to agree to the company, refuting to believe that the seat still lay vacant. Hope finally gave in to despair.

"Yeh na thi humari qismat ke visaal-e yaar hota:
Agar aur jeete rehte yahi intezaar hota."

It was not destined that I should meet my beloved
The same wait would have tormented me had I lived a little more.

She began her mehfil with a carefully chosen ghazal of Ghalib. She addressed the Kotwal next:

"Ye kahan ki dosti hai ke bane hain dost naaseh?
Koi chara-saaz hota, koi gham-gusaar hota.

What has friendship come to when friends are tormentors,
how I wish for a healer, for a sympathizer.

Koi mere dil se puchhe tere teer-e neem-kash ko
Ye khalish kahan se hoti jo jigar ke paar hota.

Ask not my heart about your half-hearted shot,
it would not have ached had it traversed across.

Kahun Kis se main ke kya hai, shab-e gham buri bala hai
Mujhe kya bura tha marna agar ek baar hota."

Whom shall I confide in the pains of a night of sorrow,
Death wouldn't have bothered me had it just been once.

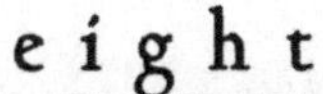

eight

I

"IT'S BEEN OVER A year now, Shams...you had said that Brit...what's his name—yes, William Frazer—would help you," Ghalib said as he strolled out of the inn with Shams in tow.

"I'll kill him, swear on god, I'll kill him," Shams said, adjusting the sling on his arm, his face livid with rage.

A man groomed the two horses tied to a mango tree in the foreground.

"First of all, do not swear on god for all trivial things," Mirza looked up at Shams, "and if you do, swear for something good."

Shams kept quiet, and Mirza said further, "What happened to that Haji—he did not reach my money to Yusuf!"

"He ran away with my money too," Shams tried to offer a poor consolation. "He disappeared six months ago."

"What about the petition that you made me sign?" Ghalib enquired.

"Frazer said that he has sent it to Calcutta—to General Metcalfe—he is the one who sits on the verdict now..." he trailed off into a silence.

"Yes, what was it that you wanted to say?" Ghalib goaded him.

"Asad Bhai, it seems that we have to make a trip to Calcutta," Shams said reluctantly.

"So you have plans to go to Calcutta?" Ghalib enquired.

"No, not me, I do not have the strength to. The onus of Arif's adolescent children is on me—had it not been for the responsibility of Yusuf Miyan that you are shouldering, I would have asked you to..."

Mirza remained quiet.

Shams asked again, "Well, forget it, how's *bhabhi*?"

"Umrao. She's fine. Expecting again! Allah granted her children but grudged them lives, she's more careful this time—been to every place of worship, sought blessings of every saint and fakir—asks me to offer a *chaddar* at the grave of the saint."

They arrived near the horses, mounted them, bid adieu to each other and galloped away.

2

"*Hazrat*," Wafadar addressed the two men at Mirza's doorstep, "Mirza Saheb has gone to Mehrauli, he may be a little late in returning—I will let him know that you had come—his estate is about to be restored."

"We want our dues cleared not his estate. Ask Mirza to come and clear his dues at the shop. We do not like to give so many reminders," the grocer said and left. But the draper still stood there and was joined by Fiddan who stood a little away hiding himself from the door.

"You too may go, Sayyed Saheb!" Wafadar addressed the draper. "You won't achieve anything by harassing a poet."

"Where am I harassing him, Bibi? It was you who had asked me to come today," the draper said.

"But how was I to know that he would be off to Mehrauli right in the morning?" Wafadar said.

"When shall I come again?" the draper asked.

"I'll talk it out with *Huzoor* and shall let you know. Good-bye."

She turned and went in. The draper too turned only to confront Mirza approaching the house. He stopped and greeted him.

"*Adaab*, Sayyed Bhai, what brings you here?" Mirza said.

"Wafadar had bought some cloth, last month. Begum had asked for it to have your cloak stitched..."

"Wasn't I enough to solicit for debts," Mirza smiled, "that Begum too now has begun to borrow..."

"But I was told..." Sayyed butted in.

"Sayyed Saheb!" Mirza did not let him finish his sentence, "a good enough pension used to fall my share, it has been stalled. You do know the advocate, Hiralal —he is pleading my case. I'll meet him today and talk about the matter..."

"Don't embarrass me Mirza," the draper butted in once again, "I hadn't come to remind you; I wouldn't have been here in the first place had I not been called—Goodbye!" saying this he left. Mirza turned saying,

"Qarz ki pite the mae, lekin samjhte the ke haan
Rang laegi humari faqa masti ek din."

Goblets we toasted in debt
Aware that it would show results one day.

But before he could step into the house, Fiddan stepped out from the shadows and greeted him. Mirza replied silently, touching his forehead. Fiddan bowed again and offered a letter. It read:

"Tum jano tum ko ghair se jo rasm-O-raah ho
Mujh ko bhi poochte raho tho kya gunah ho"

You keep an account of your love of another
Let not it be a crime to ask after me!

Ghalib pushed the letter in his pocket and said,

"Wafa kaisi? Kahan ka ishq? jab sar phorna thhera
To phir, ae sang-dil, tera hi sang-e aastan kyun ho?"

If I need bang my head, talk not of love, of faith
Why must be it at your threshold, at your petrified heart.

And he finally stepped into the innards of his house. Fiddan looked at him dispappearing into the shadows of the house and moved away into the *gali,* reciting over the couplet,

"Wafa kaisi? Kahan ka ishq? ..."

3

Nawabjaan's eyes were moist even as the bangle-seller put on the glass bangles on her wrists. She softly hummed,

"To phir, ae sang-dil, tera hi sang-e aastan kyun ho?"

"Whose lyrics are you humming?" her mother asked as she came to the threshold.

Another bangle cracked and Rukmini, the bangle-seller burst in with apologies, "No *bibi,* no, it's not your hand that's stiff—only my bangles are cheap and have not the courage to be beauty of your arms."

"You make beautiful talk, Rukmini *tai,*" Fiddan remarked.

"*Aye Hai!*" Rukmini commented, "I do not resemble your aunt by any stretch of imagination."

Nawabjaan did not appreciate this small talk.

"You may go, Fiddan," Nawabjaan said, "come after some time. Whenever Rukmini is here, you keep hovering around."

Fiddan headed for the stairs and was caught by Nawabjaan's warning, "And don't you go and find a cushion for yourself in the smoke house or else it would be days before we catch a glimpse of you."

Fiddan looked at Rukmini and exchanged a smile as he went down. She once again engaged herself in putting the bangles on Nawabjaan's wrists as she leaned against the door and hummed:

"Wafa kaisi? Kahan ka ishq? jab sar phorna thhera
Tho phir, ae sang-dil, tera hi sang-e aastan kyun ho?"

If I need bang my head, talk not of love, of faith
Why must it be at your threshold, at petrified heart.

Nawabjaan's voice was laced with sadness. It brought her mother out again.

"Whose lyrics have captivated you thus?" she asked.

Nawabjaan smiled without lifting her head.

Malka answered the question herself, "Mirza Ghalib, isn't it?"

Nawabjaan smiled in affirmation.

"Your attraction towards Ghalib doesn't find favour with the Kotwal," her mother said.

"He does not own me in anyway. I am not his bought slave," Nawab replied under her breath.

"Nobody is his bought slave, dear—but he has a stranglehold over the city."

"So?" Nawabjaan replied angrily.

"I hope he doesn't trouble the poor poet because of you," Malka said.

On hearing this, Nawabjaan became pensive.

4

Mirza Ghalib sat with his lawyer in his house, sprawled comfortably on the *diwan*.

"How will you repay all these debts, Mirza? You spend recklessly and you borrow without any thought. How will you fight these cases?" Hiralal expressed anguish at the situation but Mirza maintained a calm exterior.

"On the one hand, Mathura Das is getting a decree on you, on the other, is a long line of creditors and the pension on your estate—there is no sign of settlement. God only knows when your pension will be reimbursed..."

"If God was to give a verdict, Hiralal," Mirza chipped in, "then what would an advocate do? I had entrusted this case into your hands in the hope that you would get me my share."

"And my share, when shall I get it?" Hiralal asked with a smile.

"The entire ghazal was well said, Hiralal," Mirza answered with a smile, "but for this concluding couplet. Get me my pension and take your share. The pleading is your work. Keep me for signing the document. If you ask me to write panegyrics I will—I shall praise the *haakim* in my verses, the rest is your work."

As he got up to leave. Har Gopal Tufta entered, "Greetings Mirza, where are you off to?"

"This was the safest haven of all but now even Hiralal has begun to ask for his fees! Goodbye!" and he left.

Tufta occupied Ghalib's place on the *diwan*, "Hiralal, I haven't seen another man like him. He has a ten stone heart in an eight stone body."

"But we cannot make things work with our heart, Bhai Hargopal. We do need to rack our brains—from ten thousand his pension was reduced to five and from five to three. And now all he gets is eighty two rupees and eight annas—his relatives have stolen everything. And Mirza, the real inheritor of the state, was left with a pittance."

"Is there any hope of getting something?" Tufta enquired.

"If he gets everything, he will play in riches and if not, he will spend his life in bankruptcy."

"But is there a possibility?"

"It all depends on the will of Company Bahadur. Truth is, there's no power left in the hands of the king emperor."

"But I ask, is there hope of him getting something?" Tufta repeated his question, the third time.

"In my belief, only General Metcalfe can do something and he is in Calcutta these days."

"So should he go to Calcutta?"

"Hmm!" Hiralal paused for a while and then nodded his head, "he needs to."

5

Fiddan made his way through a dark, dingy street lined with gamblers, clutching desperately onto a small cloth bag. He crossed them and climbed an oldish wooden staircase. He was halfway on the stairs when the police raided the street. He paused, looked at the running crowd, the gamblers caught by the police. Puzzled, he suddenly jumped down the stairs only to fall on the street. The mouth of his clothbag gaped open to throw the gold ornaments he had kept close to his heart.

"My jewels...," Fidden shouted as he stopped to pick them. The hands of a policeman caught him by the collar.

"Swear on god...swear on god, they are my jewels, I wasn't gambling... they are my jewels and I am not lying." Fiddan protested. But before he could complete the sentence, the policemen pushed him forward.

6

Fiddan staggered, stumbled and stood quiveringly in front of the Kotwal.

"So you too were gambling," the Kotwal shouted at him in rage.

"You know me...I do not gamble. I have been unnecessarily..." Fiddan fumbled at his words.

"And whose jewels are these?" the Kotwal asked sternly and then examined the jewels.

Fiddan was speechless.

"Where were you taking them?"

"Se...Se...," Fiddan couldn't bring himself together to complete his sentence.

"Off to sell them?"

"No," he shook his head.

"Who had sent you?"

Fiddan was silent.

"Who? Nawabjaan?"

"No, not her."

"Then, her mother?"

He shook his head vehemently, "No!"

"Then who?" there was doubt in the Kotwal's voice this time, "did you steal them?"

Fiddan could merely stare, helplessly.

"So you steal too. You thief, you druggy!" the Kotwal flared up and slapped him.

7

"He didn't steal. He's not a thief, leave him," Nawabjaan appealed.

"Do not lie," the Kotwal said. "Fiddan himself has admitted to his crime."

"I had asked him to—sent him to sell the jewels," she added emphatically, "to Seth Sukhchain." He took a deep breath, dropped his tone and said, "What befell you to sell off the jewels?"

"There was a need. I had to repay someone's debt."

"Whose?"

"Why are you bothered? It doesn't concern you." she looked up angrily.

The Kotwal strolled away and then abruptly turned, "So, now I understand—Seth Sukhchain! Isn't he the one who's about to bring a decree against Ghalib?"

8

The evening brought in scores of devotees to the dargah. Outside, a large crowd thronged the shops selling flowers, garlands, coloured *chaddars* and caps.

Ghalib passed a veiled woman when she called after him, "Mirza!"

He stopped and looked around.

"*Adaab* Mirza!" the woman spoke from behind the veil, "you didn't come over the other evening—I waited long for you. Even my hennaed hands have faded in your wait. Look at them," she extended her palms for him to see.

Ghalib's name on her plam had paled. He watched them in silent admiration. She added, "Look at them, their complexion has dulled ever since."

Mirza said in reply.

"Tha zindagi mein marg ka khatka laga hua
Urne se peshter bhi mera rang zard tha."

The fear of death was constant in life time.
Pale was my complexion even before it would fade.

"Wonderful! Where shall my admiration cease? Every single verse of yours takes away my life," she paused and then added, "and how are you here? I had heard..."

"Come to offer a *chaddar* on the grave, Nawabjaan." Ghalib said.

She felt ecstatic, as she heard her name pronounced by his lips, for the first time. She sighed. "Allah!"

He added, "I have come to ask for the blessing of life for somebody."

"I have come to pray for somebody's success in life," she said

Ghalib smiled faintly and recited:

"Aah to chahiye ik umr asar hone tak!"

A life for a wish to come true.

"My saint has granted me my every wish and I am sure that he will grant me this one too. You will see, one day my poet shall be the poet laureate of this city."

"And if this wish of yours be granted, I shall personally come to present you a shawl in your very home."

"You will come then?" she asked impatiently, "once, just once!" her voice choked as she pleaded.

"Yes, most certainly," Ghalib promised with a nod.

Nawabjaan took her seat in the *tonga* and as it gathered speed her voice echoed against the reply:

"Ishq mujh ko nahin, wehshat hi sahi,
Meri wehshat, teri shohrat hi sahi.

Hum bhi dushman to nahin hain apne,
Ghair ko tujh se muhabbat hi sahi.

Hum koi tarke wafa karte hain,
Nah sahi Ishq, musibat hi sahi."

If not love let craziness be my lot
And my lot be your pot of fame.

Ill-wisher I am not of my ownself
What if, if another desires you.

I am not foregoing my love for you
Be it my aches if you take it otherwise.

nine

I

"KISI KO DE ke dil koi navasanj-e-fughan kyun ho
Nah ho jab dil hi seene mein tho phir mounh mein zaban kyun ho."

Why must you lament after you give away your heart?
If the heart not be with you, why must the tongue wail?

Nawabjaan hummed the ghazal with great emotion. She had sprawled herself carelessly on her cot, her hair, long tresses of silk, drooped down the bed. 'Mushata' sat behind, running a comb through her hair. Her song rose in short spasms, and seemed to have developed a strange attraction to the singer. The tune hovered about her as painful notes of unrequited love. Suddenly, her tune was picked up on the sarangi. It filled the room and managed to break the frowns on Nawabjaan's face into a smile.

"There's magic in his hands," Nawabjaan remarked spontaneously about Namichand's ability to play the sarangi.

"What did Mirza say? Will he ever come or does he intend to keep trying your patience?" Mushata smiled and asked.

Nawabjaan sang the next couplet of the ghazal in reply,

"Yahi hai azmana, to satana kis ko kehte hain
Adu ke ho liye jab tum, tho mera imtehan kyun ho!"

If this be your test, what must your torment be?
If you change your allegiance over to my rival, why must you test me?

The reply careened out of the window and dropped down to Haji Mir's bookshop, where Ghalib sat engrossed in a book. The faint note of the ghazal tapped on his shoulders and he looked up. The rays of the setting sun reddened his face. He looked at Haji Mir who smiled at him, "Mir Saheb," Ghalib enquired of him, "I had given her just one couplet, who reached the others to her?"

"Bhai! She's an admirer of yours," Mir Saheb said. "When she asks me for your verses, I can't refuse. Umpteen times in a day she enquires after your health and I don't get tired to tell her your state...."

The notes of another couplet made Mir Saheb pause in between:

"Qafus mein mujh se rudad-e chaman kehte na dar hamdam
Giri hai jis pe kal bijli, woh mera ashyan kyun ho."

Don't be scared to tell a caged me, the state of the garden
why must the nestle be mine, where a lightening struck yesterday.

Ghalib shut the book he was engrossed in and stood up to leave.

"Where to?" Haji asked.

"I do not trust my steps, Mir Saheb. "Am scared that I may tread on to a path in which I myself become a pirate. Scared that I may rob myself one day." He bid adieu to his friend and left the shop. Only the sounds of his tender calf skin shoes were left behind.

Haji took a puff of his *hukka* and stared at Mirza, black cloaked, still visible in the gathering darkness. Hardly had Mirza left that Fiddan appeared. "Greetings, Mir Saheb," he said. Haji took another drag at his pipe but it was extinguished now.

"Nawabjaan is enquiring," Fiddan continued, "if Mirza Ghalib had come over here or will he come?...or if there is any message from him?"

Haji looked up at him. The darkness of the evening was gathered in the white of his eyes.

Mushata was still occupied in combing Nawabjaan's hair. She would strike up bits of conversation with her. A soul stirring tune sprang out of Namichand's sarangi.

"Mirza doesn't seem to be such a faithful," Mushata said.

"Wafa kaisi? Kahan ka ishq? jab sar phorna thhera,
To phir, ae sang-dil, tera hi sang-e aastan kyun ho?"

If I need bang my head, talk not of faith of love
and why must it be at your threshold, at your petrified heart?

Nawabjaan's eyes were downcast and as her lips trembled to give life to the ghazal, her eyes bathed in the pains of labour. Not far away, the eyes of Namichand too welled up with tears and he pulled a sorrowful, lonesome *alaap* on his sarangi.

2

Ghalib sat on a long bench outside Nanbai's shop. The late afternoon sun had brought life out on the streets. There were numerous people huddled in clusters on benches. A shoemaker sat on the ground next to Ghalib, fitting a shoe on his foot.

"I asked many," the shoemaker Bhola said, "to tell me the way to your house. I told them that I had sold many a pair of shoes to you in Agra but there wasn't any among God's faithful...."

"I have no objection with God's faithfull, Bhola Nath. You would have done better had you endeavoured to seek my address from Nanbai. I am not Asad here, but I've earned ill repute under the name of Ghalib,"

"*Arrey bhai,* these shoes bite a lot," another of Bhola's customer complained as he tried on a pair.

"Now, *Hazrat,* if you push your foot in the mouth of a shoe, it will but bite, what else?"

"Pretty ill mannered, aren't you?" the customer said, offended.

"Don't take offence," Ghalib interferred, "though he is a bit cheeky he makes excellent shoes."

"And, Saheb," Bhola couldn't stop himself from commenting, "Agra's shoes do pretty well in Dilli, ask Asad *bhai,*" he looked mischieviously at Ghalib.

"But only the shoes," Ghalib commented.

"*Arrey* Mirza Saheb," a man sitting next to Ghalib nudged him, "he's coming."

"Who is coming, *bhai*?" Ghalib turned to him.

"Ustad Zauq is coming in a palanquin."

A palanquin entered the lane and approached the idlers at the shop.

"In great pomp and splendour is he coming into this lane," one said.

"Knows not he in whose lane he has stepped in," another said.

"He's in Nausha Miyan's lane," another exclaimed.

The palanquin was almost parallel to them when Ghalib threw up a verse on Ustad Zauq,

"Hua hai shah ka masahib, phire hai itrata."

Put on airs, since he's become the king's courtier.

"*Wah, Wah,* Mirza," the people gathered around him hailed his verse.

"Hua hai shah ka masahib, phire hai itrata."

Ghalib's words were packed with calculated measures of sarcasm, his cup of tea still held in one hand.

The group picked up his line and repeated it over and over again with reckless abandon, till they felt they had crashed the roof of Zauq's palanquin.

Zauq paused, cast a glance at the gathered crowd, stroked his beard and then ordered the palanquin bearers to move ahead. The gang of idlers broke out in laughter that grew taking within in its folds the entire crowd.

3

Zauq stood leaning against a pillar looking down the street. He stood there motionless, staring blankly at the pedestrians. Several of his disciples were scattered in the room in conference.

"*Arrey* Saheb," one said, "he is not fit to move in the company of kings and has the audacity to comment on Ustad."

"A pretty mean act, Mirza did," the other said.

"Don't you remember the day when he ran out of the *mushaira* with his tail between his legs," another one added.

Zauq paced up and down the room, his hands clasped behind him. "There's a *mushaira* this coming Friday. Call him over to the fort then. He will be humiliated completely."

"Why the hell will he come to the *mushaira*? Doesn't he know the king emperor will have him thrown out of the gathering?"

After listening to the conversation intently, Zauq said, "Send him an invitation—and Yaas, don't forget to mention the incident to Abu Zafar."

4

"I want you to take me to the church," said the Britisher who was dressed in his Sunday best, barely putting together bits and pieces of Urdu to convey the message to his coachman. His wife stood next to him.

"No, Saheb," the coachman said, "why don't you try and understand, I do not know any church-vurch, and I won't go."

"Church means *girija*!" the Britisher rummaged through his stock of Urdu words to find an equivalent for his place of worship.

"*Arrey* Bhai, *girija* or *uthja*, what do I have to do with it? I am tired. I want to rest. Ask your wife to get down from the carriage," the coachman said to the Britisher, indicating towards his wife who had managed to clamber on to the carriage.

By now, an assortment of people had gathered around the two trying to explain things out. The Britisher, finding himself at a loss, recognized an aquaintance from a sea of faces. "*Aye*, Maulvi Saheb," he addressed him, "tell this man, make him understand that me, my wife, my family..." an excitement gripped him, "we want to go to church, ask him to take us to church."

"Maulvi Saheb," the coachman too found a mediator in the clergy, "ask him to go to the next crossroad and hire another *tonga*—I have been travelling from four and I have reached Delhi only now. I am tired and my horse needs rest more than I. He can't move."

"Biddu Miyan," the Maulvi said, "these are *firangi* people, don't antagonize them, they will unnecessarily create a ruckus...."

"Why don't they do it in Englisthan," the coachman was vexed, "why do it here? Does this land belong to their fathers?"

The import of the coachman's English did manage to cross the language barrier; the Britisher flared up and he started saying, "What did you say? Whom did you call my father.........?"

The coachman suddenly broke his stick into two and pushed him away.

"Darling, Darling...," the Britisher's scared wife said meekly.

"I kill you...idiot. I'll kill this bloody *tongawala*, kill you." A few people inched forward to enjoy the altercation. Maulvi Saheb held Biddu Miyan firmly, who too by now had lost his temper.

"Leave me, Maulvi Saheb," he said, "leave me, give way, I won't leave the man," and a fist fight ensued. Some of the people butted in to drag the two apart.

"Get out from here," Maulvi Saheb counselled Biddu Miyan. "Leave here before a riot breaks out with the Britishers."

"Let it be," the coachman said still agitated. "How many of these whites are here? I'll roast them all."

"You don't know who I am," the Britisher said, trying to free himself from the grasp of the people. "I am William Frazer, I'll kill you, you idiot... Leave me... Leave me, you bastard. I'll see him," the man said in a burst of uncontrolled, unreigned rage. His wife stood away from the crowd, trembling.

"Take this white to the mosque," one commented, "and make him recite the Kalma... and be a Sunni!"

"Yes, please," another commented.

"Leave me," said the Britisher.

"Go away, Biddu Miyan, go away," the Maulvi said again. The coachman, his rage now in control, realized the gravity of situation and harnessed his horse to the carriage. "Maulvi Saheb, will you do me a favour? Reach a message to Mirza Nausha—I had brought Bansidhar from Agra yesterday..."

"Don't you worry about it," Maulvi Saheb assured him, "I'll see to it."

Biddu climbed into his *tonga* and rushed away through the bazaar.

5

"Whenever you come, Lala, you bring luck with you," Mirza Ghalib said as he unrolled a royal invitation. "Look here, you came over yesterday and today once again, I've received an invitation from the king emperor, sent by Ustad Zauq."

"Congratulations, my friend!" Bansidhar said as he shook hands with his friend. "I always knew it, for how long will a goat avoid the slaughter of the kid."

Ghalib whispered in a tone laced with secrecy, "Tell me, between the king emperor and the poet-laureate, who's the goat and who's the kid?" And they both laughed. The cat looked up at the two friends from a saucerful of milk and cleaned her whiskers.

"But still, you be careful," Bansidhar said. "Ustad Zauq would not let you set your feet firmly in the court."

6

The Diwan-e-Aam, the hall of the people, bristled with life even while darkness took it in its fold. Zafar sat on a throne in the center. The audience of some poets sat around him, with Zauq in his immediate vicinity, and Ghalib next to Mufti Sadruddin.

"We are thankful to all the poets and lovers of poetry who are here in this gathering," Zafar said. "Before the *mushaira* commences, I want to make it clear that our Ustad Sheikh Ibrahim Zauq is poet laureate of the king. Some of you have taken the liberty to pass comments on him in public; which is not becoming of their stature. I hope that such frivolous levity will not be indulged in hereafter, and people must not cross the limits of nobility."

The gathering was taken aback with the king emperor's utterance. Azurda, on behalf of the gathered poets remarked, "No, *huzoor*, there is not any one among us capable of taunting Ustad Zauq thus, none of us will consent to such breach of etiquette."

"But Mirza Nausha did," Yaas immediately blurted, "on a busy road, he did taunt Ustad Zauq and said..." he stopped midway. Everybody looked at Ghalib.

"What did he say?" Azurda asked.

"Said he has put on airs since he's become the king's courtier."

There was a loud murmur in the crowd and Zauq sat with a complacent look on his face counting the beads of his pearl necklace.

"Is it true, Mirza Nausha?" the king emperor wanted to know.

"Yes, *huzoor*," Mirza Ghalib admitted, "It's true—it is the first verse of the concluding couplet of my new ghazal."

Zauq let the necklace go from his hand. The expression on his face was reduced to one of curiosity. The gathered audience looked around at each other.

"Would you recite the couplet, Sir?" Azurda asked again.

"Hua hai shah ka masahib, phire hai itrata."
Put on airs since he's become the king's courtier,

Ghalib recited, looked towards Zauq and repeated the couplet.

"Hua hai shah ka masahib, phire hai itrata."
Put on airs since he's become the king's courtier,

he shifted his gaze to Azurda and completed the couplet,

"Varna shehar mein Ghalib ki abru kya hai."
Or else what was Ghalib's reputation worth in the city.

"*Wah!* Beautiful, wonderful, Mirza," a compliment spontaneously escaped Azurda's lips. The king emperor looked at Zauq who added,

"If the closing verses are so beautiful, what must the entire ghazal be like. We must hear it."

"Mirza," Zafar addressed Ghalib, "would you care to please recite the ghazal? Let tonight's session begin with this ghazal of yours."

"The light of the evening, the Sham-e-Mehfil be brought before Mirza

Asad Ullah Khan Ghalib." An announcement was thus, made. A liveried attendant placed a lit lamp before Ghalib.

Mirza cleared his throat, fumbled around in his pocket, took out a piece of paper and sought Zafar's permission to recite the ghazal.

"Har ek baat pe kehte ho tum, ke tu kya hai."
On the turn of every phrase you doubt my entity,

he recited.

"Har ek baat pe kehte ho tum, ke tu kya hai."

The assembled poets picked up his verse.

"Tumhi kaho ke ye andaz-e guftagu kya hai."

Tell me after what fashion have you chiselled this tete-e-tete

Ghalib recited further. The gathering burst into an applause as did Zafar.

"Ragon mein daurte phirne ke hum nahin qael,
Jab aankh hi se na tapka to phir lahoo kya hai."

Worthy not of running in the veins,
the blood that does not trickle down the eyes.

Ghalib moved on to the next couplet.

The Diwan-e-Aam echoed with an appreciation of Ghalib. Even Ustad Zauq joined in. Mufti stole a glance towards the piece of paper that Ghalib held in his hand but only a blank sheet greeted him. He looked at Ghalib and smiled. Ghalib winked at him in acknowledgement.

"Encore! Encore!" the gathering said. Ghalib recited his verse again.

"Ragon mein daurte phirne ke hum nahin qael,
Jab aankh hi se na tapka to phir lahoo kya hai."

Worthy not of running in the veins,
the blood that does not trickle down the eyes.

7

Hafiz turned into the gate singing. He clanged his tongs together to provide rhythm to the next couplet,

"Chipak raha hai badan par lahoo se perahan
Hamari jeb ko ab hajat-e rafu kya hai."

When the cloth glues to the body with sweat
why must the cape need tailoring.

"Jala hai jism jahan, dil bhi jal gaya hoga."

Where the body's consumed in the fire,
the heart too must have been burnt.

8

Nawabjaan sang accompanied by Namichand on his sarangi.

"Jala hai jism jahan, dil bhi jal gaya hoga
Kuredte ho jo ab rakh, justuju kya hai?"

Where the body's consumed in the fire,
the heart too must have been burnt,
what may you wish now for the ashes to yield.

"Har ek baat pe kehte ho tum...," she stressed the refrain.

"Rahi na taqate guftar, aur agar ho bhi
To kis umeed pe kahiye ke aarzoo kya hai."

The body's sapped of the power to speak, and even
if there may be on what hope may I say what my desire is.

ten

I

THE EVENING SEEMED darkened in the smoky *chandukhana* and the crowd pulling at their pipes made the atmosphere more heavy. As one left, another entered.

"So you have come back again! Haven't you just been out?" Khurshid addressed the newcomer who had tapped on his knee as soon as he spotted him.

"I'd forgotten to ask what day it was today," Auj said.

"Thursday, why?"

"When was the *mushaira*?"

"Which one? Mirza Ghalib's?"

"*Wah,* miyan! You never liked to take the name of that man from Agra on your lips earlier, now you attribute the whole *mushaira* to his genius."

"What can I say, Auj *bhai*.Yaas Miyan made me promise not to utter a word in his praise, but what could I do? Praise spontaneously escaped my lips."

Another man joined their conversation. As soon as Khurshid finished his confession he said, "I haven't ever seen such a *mushaira* before at the fort. The king emperor was so bewitched..."

"I too tried to exercise control over myself," Khurshid whispered his confession, "but when Ustad Zauq himself began to praise him, I too..." He slapped Auj on his thighs and exuberantly said, "Auj *bhai*! Let us smoke another another chilam to Ghalib's health. Now he too is a Dilliwala."

2

"Ho ga koi aisa bhi ke Ghalib ko na jane."

Must there be someone who knows not who Ghalib is.

Zafar recited as he walked a few paces with the poet laureate.

"Shayer to achha hai par badnam bahut hai."

Yes Sir, a good poet he is, but steeped deep in ill repute,

Zauq added and they both broke out in peels of laughter. However, Zafar brought himself to say, "Are not these verses said in his own praise by Mirza Nausha? There would hardly be any poet in Dilli who does not know him."

"Not only poets, huzoor-e-wala, but gamblers, alcoholics, money, lenders, must there be someone who knows not who Ghalib is."

Zafar smiled albeit weakly, "Miyan Fakhru, my eldest son, has expressed the desire to enlist himself as a disciple of Mirza Ghalib." Zauq looked shyly at Zafar but kept his silence to ask again, "What do you think of Ghalib?"

"A good poet, nonetheless..." Zauq said with smile.

"But steeped deep in ill repute," Zafar completed his sentence and laughed lightly.

"Not fit to move in royal company," Zauq added, "and Prince Fakhru is at an impressionable age — quite vulnerable to pick up bad habits of gambling and boozing. There's hardly any money lender in the city to whom Ghalib is not indebted. He has never recited his namaz, never kept his rozas and when asked says,

"Jis paas roza khol kar khane ko kuch na ho
Roza agar na khaey to lachar kya kare."

The one who has not food to break his fast upon,
if he feasts not on his is fasts what else.

But Zafar had a different view, "Hasn't Hazrat Ali Razi Allah Unnah said:

"Kya gham hai uss ko jis ka Ali sa imam ho
Itna bhi aey falak zada kyun be-hawas hai."

When you have the lord Hazrat Ali preacher,
why must o' you heaven born be so worried.

"When and how did he come to be a Shia no one knows," Zauq commented, "for his father and his mother were both Sunnis."

"Must have been in the influence of Mullah Abdulsmath," Zafar said. "Perhaps, he was under his tutorship at the age of thirteen or fourteen."

They both sat down.

"But I believe it's not fair to know of a poet's faith from his verses," Zafar said.

"Yes Sir, if he does have any faith," Zauq did not miss an opportunity to taunt.

"Ghalib did not come after that *mushaira*. Perhaps Miyan Fakhru was impressed by him then. I think a message ought to be sent to his home.."

"Yes Sir, a message ought to be sent to his home or .... perhaps to his gambling den," Zauq said, hitting out again.

3

The happy notes of a mellifluous song filled Mirza's house. Women dressed in their festive best filled in the inner courtyard. Someone pounded the tout skin of the *dholak*, and another sang to its tune — a song sung for the wellbeing of a child. Even Umrao joined in with a tune here and tap there. Young, tender feet pounded the entire house. A maid brought in a little boy, dressed in robes fashioned after his father and the gathering of the women burst out laughing at his sight.

"This robe has come from Lala Bansidhar. I believe his wife stitched it with her very own hands," a lady in the gathering commented.

"That's right," Bansidhar's wife said, "in the absence of any measurements, I kept his height in my mind and stitched it."

"Take him upstairs to his father," someone suggested.

"Yes, please do so and tell him that the son has the father's looks."

"Yes, and it is better to limit it to his looks. God forbid if he takes after his habits," someone commented.

"What's wrong with his habits, madam? By God's grace he's a good poet and now all of Dilli accepts it," Bansidhar's wife commented.

"Ask Umrao if she's happy with his habits," the lady said.

"And why not? I'm proud of him," Umrao said.

"Yes, you may be proud of him, but his pride isn't any good," the woman laughed.

"Wafadar, take this little man to his father," Umrao ordered.

Upstairs, Mirza Ghalib sat with Bansidhar and a few other friends reciting couplets from the rhymes he had written for his son:

"Tegh ka Hindi agar talwar hai,
Farsi pagri ki bhi dastar hai,"

If the Hindi for 'teg' is 'talwar'
the Persian for 'pagri' is 'dastar'.

He looked at his friends and recited further.

"Nevla ramo hai, aur taous mor
Kubuk ko Hindi mein kehte hein chakor."

If 'Nevla' os 'rasu' and 'taus' - 'mor,'
the Hindi for 'kubuk' is chakor.'

"Great, Mirza," Mufti Saheb commented, "Wonderful rhymes! Why don't you write some more for children, they will fall for your language."

"Yes, only they will! I am fed up with the grown ups," Mirza said in good humour. Laughter engulfed the room as Wafadar appeared at the door and said. "May I and Chote Miyan come in your presence, Sir?"

"Please do and you too, Chote Miyan," Ghalib answered.

Wafadar entered the room adjusting her dupatta and said, "Greetings Sir. Greet them, Chote Miyan."

Numerous hands reached out for the little Nausha.

"Doesn't he look like Mirza Nausha?" Bansidhar said fondly.

"And Nausha should be his nom de plume," Tufta commented.

"*Arrey* Miyan, why don't you recite his verse for him?" Hiralal added.

Ghalib picked up his son, put him on his lap and recited,

"Asp jab Hindi mein ghora naam pae
Taziyana kyun na kora naam pae."

If 'asp' in Hindi be known as 'ghora'
why must not be 'taziyana' called kora...

The little boy became restless. "Calm down, Chote Miyan, I've written this for you," the father said and recited further,

"Cheh ko Hindi mein kahte hain kuan
Dud ko Hindi mein kahte hain dhuan."

and if 'chah' in Hindi is called 'kuan'
'dud' in Hindi is called 'dhuan'....

Everybody laughed and Wafadar peeped through the curtain. Ghalib further said:

"Azool aur arok ki Hindi dakaar
Mey sharaab aur pinewala megusaàr."

The Hindi for 'azool' and 'arok' is dakaar
'mey' 'sharaab' and 'pinewala' 'megusaar'.

The child began to cry and Ghalib turned towards the curtain that hid Wafadar and said, "So you're annoyed at the very mention of wine. You're Umrao's son after all, no influence of mine whatsoever!" Wafadar came from behind the curtains and picked up the child. She said, "What happened? Why are you so upset?"

"Nothing," Ghalib was apologetic, "I was writing verses for him in Hindi and Persian. He didn't seem to like them."

"Why not teach him Urdu? Write verses for him in Urdu," Wafadar said.

"Urdu and Hindi is the same language, the difference lies in the script," Ghalib was slightly emphatic.

"Yes, it must be regarded as one language," Bansidhar said, "it was born here in Hindustan."

"That's right," Tufta said, "the language that was spoken in military camps, lashkar, came to be known as Urdu—Urdu itself means military camps."

"Say *Khuda Hafiz,*" Wafadar nudged the boy and turned to go.

"Where are you taking him? Let him have the feel of pen and ink. If he sits with us..."

"Begum Saheba wants to take him to the *dargah,*" Wafadar said.

"From this very age?"

"Yes, to offer a *chaddar* for thanksgiving," and she left.

"I too had promised a shawl to someone," Ghalib seemed to be reminded of something.

"To whom?" Mufti enquired.

"This fame of mine is an answer to her prayers."

4

Mirza Ghalib climbed the stairs leading to Nawabjaan's house, a beautifully woven shawl in his hand. He knocked repeatedly at the curtainless door. Nobody answered his call. He then pushed the door slightly. The room was bare, stripped down to its original nakedness—the look said it all. Mirza slowly stepped in. A couple of chairs and a few cots stood like relics. Mirza noticed a couple of couplets written on the mirror. But a sound distracted him before he could read them. He looked out and saw Fiddan who had just entered the house. He looked at Mirza out of his dim eyes and rested himself against the door.

"Where's Nawab? Shifted her residence, has she?" Ghalib asked of Fiddan.

"Unable to change her fortunes, Mirza, she changed her city," Fiddan said.

"Why, what made her leave Dilli so suddenly?" Ghalib was puzzled.

"Dilli does not suit everybody, *Huzoor*. You need to be of steel to live here," Fiddan's voice had a note of bitterness. "Since the last few months the Kotwal had made it difficult for her to breathe. She'd lose control over her tongue and the Kotwal over his hands and feet. Malka tried hard to put some sense into her..."

"Malka who?" Ghalib asked.

"Nawab's mother. But Nawab, she'd lost her balance of mind in the storm, the storm of love. To tell you the truth, Mirza, it wasn't love but *junoon*." Mirza read the couplet written on the mirror:

"Ishq mujh ko nahin wehshat hi sahi
Meri wehshat teri shohrat hi sahi."

Not love but junoon be my lot
and my lot, your fame.

"Did Nawab write this?" Ghalib once again questioned.

"It's written by you, though the writing is hers. How beautifully do you tell the tales of people," Fiddan's voice tremored as he answered.

Ghalib moved to the wall. Another couplet attracted his attention:

"Qata kijiey na t'aluq hum se
Kuch nahin hai tho adavat hi sahi."

Sever not your relations with me
Be it of enemity if nothing else.

He moved towards the door as he said, "I've been a bit late, Fiddan. Nawab's debt is still on me." He opened the half closed door and found another couplet written there,

"Hum bhi tasleem ki khu daleenge
Be-niazi teri adat hi sahi."

I too shall learn to accept
Your aloofness as your habit if nothing else.

He walked out slowly and turned to say,

"Yaar se chher chali jae Asad
gar nahin vasal, tho hasrat hi sahi."

She walked away from you, Asad
Be it an unrequited desire if not union.

5

Ghalib stood against a pillar on the terrace in a solemn mood watching the rain pour out of the black night. He started humming:

"Hazaron khwahishen aesi, ke har khwahish pe dam nikle
Bahut nikle mere arman, lekin phir bhi kam nikle.

Numberless were the desires whose fulfillment I sought
But few seemed the numerous that did come true

Nikalna khuld se Adam ka sunte aae hain lekin
Buhat be aabru ho kar, tere kuche se hum nikle

I had heard of the expulsion of Adam from Paradise
But greater seemed the dishonour at my exile from your lane.

Khuda ke waste, parda na kaaba se, Utha zalim
kahin aesa na ho yan bhi, wahi kafir sanam nikle

For God's sake lift not the veil from Kaaba
What if it is unlike the face of my Kagan beloved

Kahan mae-khane ka darwaza, Ghalib! aur kahan wa'az!
Per itna jante hain, kal woh jata tha ke hum nikle."

What be the relations between a preacher and an alehouse,
But I did see him cross the threshold as I entered.

The rain began to rush down in a torrent.

eleven

I

"HOW MUCH HAVE you weighed?" Wafadar looked at her purchase and haggled with the grocer, "it seems less to me."

"Full three seers have I weighed, not a wee bit less," the grocer grumbled.

"But I had asked for five seers," Wafadar complained.

"You do not get things for the asking, lady. Look, I have been asking Mirza for my dues for over a month now," the grocer commented sarcastically.

"But we have got visitors over at our place, *bhai*, this will not suffice," she looked pitifully at the three seer of pulses.

"Be happy and satisfied with what you've got, bibi. Mirza hardly has a *cowrie* in his pocket and he goes around throwing dinner parties with the change of the breeze. His sight evokes compassion or else..."

"He will repay you," Wafadar cut him short, "do not begrudge him."

"You are pretty loyal to your master," the grocer said.

"Yes, she is his faithful, and her name's Wafadar, faithful, too," a shopper commented.

"Look at his fame, reached the skies. It has spread far and wide—become the talk of the town, but monies—there's no mention of it," the grocer complained.

"But money's not fame's maid, it does not come with fame," the other shopper added.

"And not even pulses, Miyan," the grocer said.

Wafadar picked up her purchase and walked out.

"The world's a piece of paper, dissloves in a drop of rain," the blind singing Brahmin trotted on the street. Wafadar stopped him and asked, "Baba, you have not been to our place for the last two Tuesdays. Where have you been?"

"My wife's been away, that's why I couldn't come," he answered.

"Do come the next Tuesday."

"I will," he promised and continued with his philosophy borrowed from a popular poet.

2

A group of young children had got hold of a mentally unstable man at the corner of the street. One of them pretended to be a horse and had the man sit on his back. Another found an old hat of a Britisher and put it on the man's head. Few others busied themselves with adorning the man's hat with feathers. Another brought a stick for a cane they had seen with a mounted British soldier. A few kites soared high in the sky. The whole farce seemed forceful. And having thus decorated the insane man, they began to sing in rhythm.

"Illa pilla pala ho, gore ka munh kala ho."

Fly high, O you kites
black be the face of the whites.

They followed the 'soldier' clapping and singing. Suddenly one of the children spotted Ghalib turning into the street. He cautioned the others, "Come on, let's run. Mirza's coming!" The song slackened, lost it's rhythm and fell with a thud as the boys ran away. Even the boy who was carrying the madman's burden. The rider fell after taking a few steps. By now, Mirza was close enough to help him to his feet. The man picked up the hat from the ground and put it on his head.

"Yusuf?" Mirza was shocked, "what have you done to yourself? Take off that hat!" The man seemed more concerned at the discarding of his hat than his brother's admonishings. "Yusuf," Mirza said again, "let's go in." But the man ran to pick up his hat no sooner had his brother shifted his attention elsewhere. "Come back, Yusuf! Come here!" Mirza shouted. Yusuf came back meekly and Mirza ordered him to go inside.

"*Salam walekum, Bhaijaan*!" the man greeted his brother.

"*Salaam!* Go in!" Mirza said and caught sight of a plate with uneaten food on it. "What's this? Were you having your food?" The man nodded. Mirza yelled for Kalloo at the door and asked him, "When did Yusuf Miyan come here?"

"This very morning, *huzoor!* Along with his wife and children," Kalloo said.

"Why did you let him go out of the house? Don't you know his condition?"

"He was having his food quite alright, Sir! God knows when he picked up his plate and marched outside," Kalloo answered.

"Is Begum upset?" Ghalib asked.

"Yes, now..."

"Have you seen Khan Saheb's house in the backyard of the mosque? Make provisions for Yusuf Miyan to stay there. And listen, make arrangements for my travel to Calcutta." He then directed his attention to his brother, "Come on, Yusuf!"

"Calcutta?" Kalloo was taken aback, "That far, so suddenly..."

"Yes! It is now mandatory for me to go!" Saying this he crossed the courtyard with Yusuf. Kalloo followed behind.

"Yusuf, go finish your meal! Go along with Kalloo!" Mirza directed his brother.

3

"Greetings, Mir Saheb!" Ghalib said as he entered the bookshop.

"Greetings!" Mir Saheb said.

Ghalib unwrapped the cloth bundle he was carrying and placed the sheaf of papers in front of Mir Saheb and said, "These are all my verses Mir Saheb—all that I've written so far..."

Mir Saheb looked up at Ghalib. Mirza continued, "Keep these as a collateral and give me the fare to Calcutta. It seems there can be no verdict on my pension till I personally meet General Metcalfe."

"Mirza," Mir Saheb said, "don't make me a sinner. I will not keep your verses as mortgage and I do not have sufficient money to fund your travels to Calcutta. But yes, I can make provisions till Lucknow. I have an acquaintance there who will introduce you to the Nawab, though I hear that the power is vested in the hands of the Company Bahadur. The deputy to the sultanate, Agha Mir, has sold himself to the British."

"Say, Awadh there, and Dilli here, the king emperor at the fort and the reins in Calcutta in the hands of the Company Bahadur. Somewhere a city is sold, somewhere an entire state; at places contingents of soldiers are being bought and sold. What sort of traders have found their way here? The entire country has become a grocer's domain." Ghalib said, and addng bitterly, "I did not know there was so much to sell in the household. From the conscience to the country, everything is up for sale."

A pause filled up the gap in their conversation. Mir Saheb then added, "I've heard that King Emperor Akber-e-Sani is critically ill and perhaps his eldest son, Abu Zafar, is soon to ascend the throne."

"But have you hopes of any revolution with his crowning?" Ghalib asked.

"Perhaps his point of view will be different."

"The views and patterns of behaviour of kingship here in our country has always been the same—dynastic—and we very easily become enslaved to dynasties."

"It's possible," Mir Saheb said, "that in this time of despair, perhaps Zafar may be of some use."

4

"Lucknow aane ka ba'is nahin khulta, yani
hawase ser tamasha, sow woh bhi kam hai hum ko:"

I find no reason to come to Lucknow
Perhaps I'm not inclinded to trips for pleasure.

Ghalib thought as he transversed a dense green jungle, lit by the early morning sun. He rode his horse with a steady gallop and looked behind at his co-traveller who had his luggage with him on the horse. His face mirrored a strange apprehension at his journey. A few couplets came to his rescue.

"Maqtae silsila-e shouq nahin hai yeh shehar
Azme sere najaf-O-tawfe haram hai hum ko."

There's no dearth in the city of means to amuse oneself
Perhaps I'm inclined more towards pilgrimages.

"Liye jati hai kahin ek tawaqa Ghalib
Jada rah kashish kafe karm hai hum ko"

A hope pulls you along, Ghalib
Perhaps this path is the beginning of some benevolence.

5

Ghalib sat reclining against the high back of his easy chair in the room of an inn. A meak fire yet to fight the winter occasionally leapt up from the *aatishdaan* placed next to him. A few phials of medicines were kept on a tripod. Ghalib tore open a packet of medicine and washed it down with a glass of water.

"May we come in, *huzoor-e-wala*?" someone asked after knocking at the door.

"Do come in, Ashiq Ali!" he ushered his guests in with a gesture of his hand. As Ali and Bismil entered the room, Ghalib let out a sneeze.

"Greetings, *huzoor-e-wala!*" Bismil said

"Please allow me to keep lying down," Ghalib requested after acknowledging their greetings.

"Has your health improved?" Bismil asked showing his concern.

"Yes, but a few more days till I feel fit," Ghalib said.

"*Huzoor,* why don't you grace our home with your presence? It's been two months since you've been here in this inn," Aashiq said.

"Aashiq *bhai,*" Ghalib replied, "there are so many friends here in Lucknow that if I stay at the place of one, the other will feel offended. It is better if I stay here." He sneezed again.

"But you must give an unfortunate person like me a chance to be of service to you," Aashiq entreated.

"Oh! If I let friends be of service to me, it would necessitate to keep myself in ill-health. Would you mind if I stay healthy and fit?" Ghalib skirted the issue.

"You're impossible," Bismil smiled. "Haji Mir would think I did not take care of you."

"Do me the favour of introducing me to Nawab Haider, that's all," Ghalib answered.

Aashiq Ali described the progress so far, and added, "If you may write a *qasida* in praise of the deputy..."

Ghalib cut in, "In praise of that butcher, who with the help of the Britishers has become the minister? God help me!"

"We are helpless now and we have to get our work done. Only if you could meet Agha Mir once..."

Ghalib interrupted again, "On two conditions am I ready to meet him. First, he'll rise from his seat to greet me, and second, I'll not present any tribute to him."

Aashiq and Bismil exchanged a look. Bismil explained, "We'll tell him about the tributes but..."

"...the rest may not be possible," Aashiq completed the sentence.

"Then it may not be possible for me to meet him," Ghalib said in answer.

"I shall meet his deputy this evening and then..." Aashiq said.

"A deputy's deputy?" Ghalib sarcastically said, "alright! Let me know tomorrow."

"We'll take your leave now," they both said and left.

6

Ghalib sat on his diwan, a blanket draped over his shoulders, surrounded by a number of people from Lucknow, engaged in an animated conversation.

"But you cannot say that there's no difference between the Urdu of Dilli and Lucknow," one of them said, his voice slightly louder. "For example, even 'chariots' are known differently at the two places," another said.

"Is it right to use the feminine gender for pen (*qalam*)? Lucknowwallahs use the masculine form!" yet another said.

"If a woman writes, it is feminine, when a man writes it masculine," Ghalib smiled. A laughter broke out.

"And *joote*?" someone asked.

"Mirza would say feminine if a woman wears it and masculine when a man," someone answered.

"No, Sir," Ghalib added. "Masculine, if it hits harder and feminine, if it's light." Laughter did another round. Ghalib added in a serious note as soon as the laughter subsided, "You must note, gentlemen, that every fifty miles in Hindustan the spoken language changes slightly, so it's quite justified if there's a difference. However, if two languages become different it is correct. People do not become alienated due to differences in languages.

They do not become enemies. Let there be differences in the language of Lucknow and Dilli but that does not make them enemies." The gathering was spellbound and he added further, "Mir had come to Lucknow once— Mir Taqi Mir! You did not give him a place of honour. Dejected he left Lucknow. Tell me, whose loss was it?"

A silence engulfed everyone. Aashiq Ali got up to beg leave from Ghalib, "I should be going now, Sir."

"*Khuda Hafiz*! God be with you!" Ghalib said.

"May I say something, if you will not find it unpleasant?" Aashiq asked.

"Please!" Ghalib coaxed.

"It has been quite some time here, if we do not meet the Nawab's deputy, how are you to continue your travels?"

The flickering of the fire reflected on Ghalib's face. He sighed and smiled, "A number of young men have come and sought my tutorship here in Lucknow. The tributes that they've brought will fund part of it. I'm off to Banda tomorrow, from there to Allahabad, and then to Benaras. Once I reach Benares, I'll see what provisions I can make for the rest of the journey."

"Raat din gardish mein hain saat aasman
Ho rahe ga kuchh na kuchh ghabraen kya."

As long as the seven heavens be in the firmament
something will fall to my lot, why panic.

7

Rain drenched the road. Ghalib's carriage broke the silent monotony of the long road. Somehow, he reached Banda in Bundelkhand, where he stayed for nearly six months as the guest of Nawab Zulfikar Ali Bahadur.

Ghalib's forefathers had had a warm relationship with the Nawab's family. It was through Nawab Zulfikar Ali Bahadur that he borrowed a sum of two thousand from one Amin Chand—the money to fund his further travels. By God's grace, and Nawab Saheb's hospitality and good wishes, he recovered from his illness and sought permission to leave. "Well, Mirza," the Nawab said as they walked towards the door of his haveli, "on a long trip you are. Calcutta's far away. It'll take you four to six months to reach there..."

"Right, Sir," Ghalib said. "Been nine months since I left Dilli; God knows how long it shall take to reach Benares."

"Stay the night at Chilla Tara," the Nawab advised, "and if you desire to send any messages, give my reference to the police officer there. He'll do the needful." They stopped at the stairs and Nawab Saheb reclined against the door of the haveli. He touched his forehead and bid adieu, "Write to me once you reach Allahabad. Well, Mirza, God be with you, *Khuda Hafiz*. Now I entrust you in the hands of the Lord."

"That's not done, Nawab Saheb!" Mirza said.

"Why, what happened?" Nawab Saheb was taken aback.

"The Lord entrusted me in your hands and you are sending me back to Him," Ghalib said.

"Well said!" Nawab Saheb laughed.

Nawab Saheb's laughter filled his heart. Ghalib bid adieu and retreated.

8

Ghalib stayed at Moonda for two days. After spending a night on the way, he reached Chilla Tara. The vehicle he had hired from Banda was pretty sluggish and decided to travel by boat for the rest of the way. This journey was Ghalib's longest travel. He reached Allahabad by boat, went ahead to Benares where he stayed for quite some time. It appeared that he fell in love with the city, for he wrote an *Ode to Benares* in Persian there.

9

BENARES

The evening sun coloured the river a crimson red. Ghalib stood at the edge of the ghat. His long wavy hair fell on his shoulders. A comely beard adorned his chin. And with a shawl draped across his shoulders, he looked more like a yogi at the Ganga ghats. He stood admiring the flat bottomed boats floating on the water with lamps lit on them and music *mehfils* in progress. The sounds of *thumris* and *ghungroos* filtered into his ears. He stood there mesmerized by the sight.

10

Ghalib was on his way to his place of stay through the narrow lanes of Benares.

The streets were so narrow that one had to stand flat against the wall to let another person pass. He crossed a woman in a veil. She stopped and looked back at him. He too froze in his tracks and looked at her in puzzlement. The woman walked up to him, lifted her veil and raised her hand in greeting. Ghalib acknowledged her but in silence. Finally, she said, "Mirza, you may not know me, but I do—I'm Nawabjaan's mother."

"Where's Nawabjaan? I had gone to her house in Delhi to fulfill my promise, but I couldn't meet her," Ghalib said.

"Fled the city, so scared she was of the Kotwal's threats, Mirza. We left Delhi and somehow settled here," Malka said.

"Where's Nawab? This shawl of hers I have been carrying in trust upon my shoulders ever since. I've to reach it to her," Ghalib said, impatience pushing his words out faster.

Malka remained silent.

Ghalib had an evil premonition. "Why are you so quiet?" he asked.

Malka said in a voice choked with emotion, "Till her last breath, did she remember you. Unrequited love had gored her hollow." Ghalib shut his eyes and lowered his head. His face was blank. It was Malka's sobs that made him look up. "Mirza," she said, "come to her grave once, perhaps her soul may find some solace."

"Please," Ghalib said and followed Malka as she lead the path.

II

The evening sun bathed Nawab's gravestone in crimson as Ghalib stood silently beside it. On the tombstone, the verses of a ghazal by him were etched in a stony silence:

"Ye na thi humari kismat ke visale yaar hota
Agar aur jite rahete, yahi intezar hota."

It was not destined that I should meet my beloved
The same wait would have tormented me had I lived a little more.

"Tere wade par jiye hum to ye jaan jhoot jana
Ke khushi se mar na jate agar etbar hota!"

I would've falsified this life had I lived on your promise
Died I would have in happiness, had I faith in it.

And inspite of the epitaph's stony coldness, Ghalib could hear Nawabjaan sing those lines; her lone voice emanating in *tarannum* from the bowels of the earth. The memory of an old evening at the *dargah* came back to him. "My lord grants me each of my wishes. You'll see, one day my poet shall be the poet laureate of Dilli," she had then said...

"And if this wish of yours be granted, I shall present you with a shawl, personally at your house," he had promised Nawabjaan.

"Will you come to my house, please, just once?" he could still vividly recall her excitement.

Ghalib removed the shawl from his shoulder and spread it on the grave. He then went down on his knees, in prayer. He looked up at the epitaph and the last verse caught his eyes:

"Kahon kis se mein ke kya hai, shab-e gham buri bala hai
Mujhe kya bura tha marna agar ek bar hota."

Whom shall I confide in the pains of a night of sorrow
death would not have bothered me had it just been once.

twelve

I

CALCUTTA

ON THE TWENTY-FIRST day of February 1828, Ghalib arrived in Calcutta. That very day, somebody without any formal contractor's obligations, rented out a place for him to stay in Shimla bazaar, where now stands House Number One of Bethune Row, behind the church at the corner of Maniktala street.

Ghalib paced up and down the balcony of his first floor house. He could see the courtyard where women traced festive patterns on the gound and men were sculpting idols of Goddess Kali out of clay. He smiled at them, intrigued at their craftsmanship, in spite of the paleness spread over his bearded face.

"Durga!" he shouted for the little Bengali girl.

"Coming, Baba!" the girl answered in the vernacular from somewhere in the shadows of the balcony and climbed the stairs.

"What do you want, Baba?" she looked at Ghalib straight in the eyes, with a childlike innocence.

"Baba!" Ghalib was surprised, "whom do you call Baba, my dear?" he asked.

"Father!" she said.

"You call father Baba. What do you call an old man?"

"Buddha Baba!" the girl unravelled the mystery of her tongue.

"Buddha Baba! Father is baba, and I Buddha Baba," Ghalib was fascinated. "I…I'm here for the last six months," he paused, trying to make her understand. "I…I'm…ill…and I need milk…hot milk." He offered a jar of milk and said, "Boil it for me, will you?"

"You'll have hot milk," the girl looked puzzled.

"Yes…milk…hot…I'll have medicines with it…medicines… Boil it…for me."

"Okay, baba!" the girl took the jar and disappeared down the stairs.

"Okay, baba!" Ghalib mouthed her words.

"May I?" a voice broke into his solitude and sought permission to present itself.

"Oh, do come in Sirajuddin Saheb," Ghalib smiled, "I had been waiting for you, since the morning."

"The paint on the stairs rubs off on to my hands everytime I come here; and then I need not tell people I've been to your place; they know." He laughed almost immediately.

"Please be seated," Ghalib said in between his smile. "Has any way been thought of to meet the governor general?"

"No, not yet. In fact, these English officials are being transferred so rapidly that it's even difficult to acquaint oneself with them. You have met the Persian registrar to the office, Andrew Sterling. He says that…"

"What will come of my meeting him so often, Siraj *bhai,* the matter's not in his hands," Ghalib could not hide the irritation that etched his face in fine narrow lines. He covered his face to hide his helplessness. Moments later he looked up at Sirajuddin to say, "It's been six months since I've been here and a year and a half since I left Dilli…" He got up and walked away and then slowly turned to look back at Sirajuddin, "God knows what must have become of my home! And though Gopal Tufta does write to me, but strangely enough he circumvents the affairs at my household, as if he has something to hide. Who would be making provisions for my family, the Lord only knows. The creditors would be implementing their decrees against me, Siraj *bhai.* If the verdict does not come this once, it would indeed be difficult for me to step into Dilli. How will I face my creditors?"

"Don't be disheartend, Mirza!" his visitor consoled him. "Things will be alright with the arrival of Charles Metcalfe. He's off to Malda to enter into a pact with the Marathas. I'm positive your work will be done once he's there."

Durga stepped onto the balcony holding the jar of milk at the edges, "Here, Baba, your hot milk." She handled the jar over to Mirza.

"Well done, dear!" Mirza gently patted her cheeks. "Thank you!" He put the jar down on the table. His visitor was intruigued at Mirza's efforts to converse with the girl.

"Why don't you stay on the other side of the mosque yard, Mirza?" Sirajuddin advised. "That's a Muslim locality and it'll be easier for you there. You must be finding yourself a complete stranger here."

"No, Sir, not at all," Ghalib said, "I feel absolutely at home here. Hindustan isn't merely a Muslim locality, Siraj *bhai*. Before our advent here, some people did stay here and their customs, rites and culture are much older than our birth. Have been to Benares? Have you ever seen Somnath? It's quite puzzling that when we talk about architectural wonders, all we talk about is the Taj Mahal and the Red Fort. Do buildings too have a religion? Or is that a Hindu's horse is a Hindu and a Muslim's buffalo a Muslim?"

His visitor got up to leave and stood facing Mirza. "Last fortnight I met a pretty experienced horse," he said as they started walking down the stairs. "He had changed quite a few religions. To begin with, he was with one Karim, then with one Chelaram, and thereafter with one Robert, and finally he's with one Dhanwan Singh. He was complaining about the lack of superiority in any religion. No faith made him an elephant, he stayed a horse that he was."

His visitor laughed and Ghalib continued, "This our Bengal is a pretty fascinating place, Saheb. The Bengalis live a hundred years in the past and another hundred years in the future. And a city like Calcutta, you would not find another on this earth. I swear on God, had I not responsibilities towards my family, I would have denounced everything to settle down here."

His visitor laughed again, "Wasn't it only yesterday that you wanted to desert Hindustan in favour of settling down in Iran and spend your life in the alehouses there?"

"I thought so, but don't I have the liberty to change it," Ghalib said and then added, "and that was if my pension was not awarded to me." Ghalib opened the gate for his visitor.

"Oh! That you'll most certainly get," his visitor said. "And now, I'll take your leave, Mirza. God be with you!"

"God be with you!" Ghlib shut the gate after him and turned to walk up the stairs.

2

"Kalkatta ka jo zikr kiya to aye humnashin
Ek tir mere seene pe mara ke haay haay

Mentioned Calcutta that you did, O Beloved
An arrow traversed through my heart, O beloved

Woh sabza-zar haay mu'ater ke hai gazab
Woh naaznin-e bootan khud aara ke haay haay

Wonderful are those fields of grassy green
That tender beauty adorned by charms her own, O Beloved

Sabr aazma woh un ki nigahein ke muntazir
Taqat ruba woh un ka ishara ke haay haay."

Tries your patience those inviting eyes of her. That vitality—robbing gesture of hers, O Beloved.

Ghalib stood on his balcony stroking his beard as he recited the couplets to himself. He saw two men walk towards the little girl Durga, who was engrossed in cleaning rice at the foot of the stairs that led to Ghalib's house.

"Oh, Khoki," one of the two addressed the girl in Bengali, "does one Mirja-Oshodullah-Khan-Ghaleeb stay here?"

The girl looked up from her chore and said, "No, none by that name, not here."

"Are you sure?" the second man came forward,

"Isn't this Mirja-Ali-Shaudagor's house?"

"That's so, but no one by that name."

"Are you sure?" the man asked again.

"What's the name you said?" the girl asked again.

"Mirja-Oshodullah-Khan-Ghaleeb."

"Nobody lives here, of such a difficult name," she said.

Ghalib who stood watching them laughed.

"From Dilli. He has come from Dilli," the man added.

"From Dilli, isn't it. Oh! Now I know, our Buddha Baba," the girl was happy to discover the strangers.

"What?" the man nearly shouted.

Durga walked out into the courtyard, looked up at Ghalib's balcony and said, "Buddha Baba!"

"Come up, come up. You must be looking for me. *Walekum Slaam!* My name sounds quite like rossogulla in Bengali. Come up. From here...this way," Ghalib said. The two men climbed up and Ghalib escorted them in.

"*Adaab,* Mirza!" the men greeted Mirza.

"*Adaab!*" Mirza said, "please sit. What may I do for you, gentlemen?"

"*Huzoor,*" one of them said, "there is a *mushaira* organized tomorrow night at the Suliya school. Renowned Persian poets will grace the occasion."

"Is that so?" Ghalib commented.

"Yes, Sir!" the man said.

"Who all?" Ghalib enquired

"Hazrat Qateel Saheb, Janaab Waakib Saheb and also Kifaayat Khan Saheb from Herat," the second man said.

Ghalib seemed to ponder over the information. "Mirza Saheb, you must come," the man continued, "in fact the *mushaira* has been organized in your honour, Sir,"

"Yes, Sir, that's right," the first man added.

"Yes, I will," Ghalib smiled, "but one of you will have to come to fetch me. Been here for the last eleven months but I'm yet to become familiar with the roads."

"Yes, *huzoor,* I'll come personally," the first man said. "My name's Rashid Mustafa. You are very kind to have accepted our invitation."

"You speak Bengali pretty fluently," Ghalib commented as they got up to leave.

"Well, Sir, that's my mother tongue," the man said.

"Oh! You belong to this city then!" Ghalib further said.

"Yes, Sir I do! We'll take your leave now. *Khuda Hafiz!*" the visitors said in unison.

"*Khuda Hafiz!*" Ghalib too bid them good-bye.

3

The night had come alive. A number of people were climbing the stairs. Ghalib was being escorted by the two men and was engaged in a conversation with them.

"It is the large-heartednesss of these Englishmen," the man said, "that they have opened a new department at Fort Williams College to impart education in Hindi and Sanskrit. Where they educated Muslims earlier in Urdu and Persian, they now have made provisions to teach Hindi and Sanskrit to the Hindus."

"Whoever told you that Hindi is the language of the Hindus and Urdu of the Muslims?" Ghalib said agitated. "Har Gopal Tufta and Dayashankar Nasim have the same rights over Urdu as Raskhan had over Hindi. Waris and Farid brought life to Punjabi and Amir Khusroo contributed his mite to Awadhi. This...this is a policy of divide and rule. People are being divided over religion and languages."

"But it would be better if you do not air your views here, Mirza," Sirajuddin said, "a few Englishmen are present here at the *mushaira*."

"This is the work of these Englishmen. This is no division of languages but the division of the people; never has a language ever been slave to a religion."

"But Qatil Saheb says..." the man said.

"But why must I believe that Khatri-born?" Ghalib interrupted, "who, to have his Persian accepted, had to resort to embracing Islam."

"For God's sake," Sirajuddin said, "try to understand..."

"I do understand things, Siraj *bhai*, this is a snare spread by the English," Ghalib added impatiently.

"Please..." Siraj took Ghalib aside to pacify him but he continued, his anger unabated. "All these are meant to sweep the way to the English rule..." he added and then left the gathering.

The people present broke down in unguarded whispers. "This is sheer imprudence, gentlemen, had Mirza Saheb not been our guest here..."

4

"The entire gathering was put off by your comments and a few hot-headed youths have even got posters put on walls denouncing you," Sirajuddin said the next morning as he clambered down the stairs of Ghalib's house.

"But look, there is not a single one on my wall," Ghalib quipped light-heartedly.

"You ought to see the walls of the madrassa. The entire wall is filled with posters against you."

"And what do they say?"

"The corrected syntax of your Persian verses that you had recited last night," Siraj said.

"So now I need to learn my grammar from them!"

"They seem not to be aware of your syntax."

"Let them not be. They are free to write the way they want to. Or better still, they should ape that Qatil. To write like me..."

"Listen, Mirza," Siraj said, "I'm not bothered about it. All I'm worried about is that if this incident clings on to you and if the Englishmen get to know about it...then that matter about your pensions..."

"God be my witness, Siraj *bhai*," Ghalib interrupted, "I have never been scared to voice my opinion. Only one thought troubles me. I am a guest in this city and if I offend the people here, you are bound to say that a person had come from Dilli once—shameless, imprudent—who had fought with our elders. God forbid that I become the cause of ill-repute to my Dilliwalas. That is all, Siraj *bhai*. I plead that this incident be forgotten."

Siraj laughed.

"Siraj *bhai*, I believe you are not familiar to opposition but I am only too accustomed," Ghalib said and opened the door for him. "And please, do not worry about things. Just arrange for a meeting with Charles Metcalfe at the earliest and I'll be off thereafter."

"I'll do my best," Siraj said and wished him good bye.

"*Khuda Hafiz!*" Ghalib echoed his sentiments.

5

"Go! Go away!" the British official shouted at Ghalib who sat at his desk with Siraj. He abruptly got up and continued in the same tone of anger, in fluent Hindustani. "Go back to Dilli. Go, go back. You Indians are thankless. Small mind, small heart, can't see far. You say that Hindus-Muslims are brothers? What brothers? Which brothers? Murderers. Killers. You people keep fighting. Keep murdering each other and then say that we divide you. Idiots. Fools. You can never be far-sighted."

"Sir," Siraj pleaded, "Mirza did not mean..."

"That is enough," the officer interrupted,

"I do not want to hear any more. You may take this petition to William Frazer in Dilli. You may go to your king emperor at the fort. Go to your lousy *zillae illahi*...."

Ghalib was angered no end. He got up in a huff and left the room, with Siraj right behind him.

6

On the deck of a boat on the calm waters of the river, Ghalib stood reciting a ghazal:

"Ah ko chahiye ik umr asar hone tak
Kaun jita hai teri zulf ke sar hone tak

A life-time for a wish to come true.
But who lives till the graying of our hair.

Ashiqi sabr talab aur tamanna betab
Dil ka kya rang karun khun-e jigar hone tak

Love's patient and desire restless
What must I tell my heart till it is requited.

Hum ne mana ke taghaful, na karo-ge lekin
Khak ho jaenge hum, tum ko khabar hone tak

Agreed that you'll not hold to ridicule
But to ashes will I turn till you come to know of it.

Gham-e hasti ka Asad kis se ho juz marg ilaj
Shama har rang mein jalti hai sahar hone tak."

Death will only remedy a life of misfortunes Asad.
A flame flutters in all shades till the morning comes.

thirteen

I

"THE HOUSE, BY GOD'S grace, is still where it was," Mirza said as he got down from the *tonga* and looked at his house. The *tonga* was full of his luggage—a couple of trunks and a bed-roll tied with a rope. Kalloo stepped out to carry the luggage inside. Mufti, who had been standing at the door, too walked forward to greet his friend. Ghalib then turned to Kalloo and asked, "How have you been Kalloo Miyan, and how has Begum been keeping?"

Kalloo raised his hands in gratitude of Allah.

"I heard Wafadar has gone..." Ghalib said

"She's back since she didn't find life at her village worthwhile."

"And our little man, how's he? He must be able to trot now—must be going out on walks."

Kalloo once looked at Mufti Saheb and lowered his eyes.

"What happened?" Mirza found the silence oppressive. "Things are alright with the little one, aren't they?" He picked up the cloak over his shoulders and entered the inner courtyard calling out to his wife.

And he understood everything when he saw the tears well up in the Begum's eyes. He stood there for a moment stunned, and heard her tears complain. He then went out into the courtyard to Mufti. His eyes strangely, were dry. Mufti Saheb touched him on the shoulders. He merely nodded.

"Have patience, Mirza!" Mufti offered his consolation. "It's all His will. What He wants, what He wills—none knows—His ways are hidden..."

Ghalib blurted out in anguish."What's hidden, Mufti Saheb? I had a son—he has died, and stays buried in a grave. A wee bit soul under tonnes of earth, so much so that he can't even turn. What's the secret, what's so strange about it? Umrao Begum gave birth to him and Allah killed him. Who else can? Who else has the right?"

Mufti quoted ohe of Ghalib's verse.

"Jaan di, di hui ussi ki thi
Haq to ye hai ke haq, ada na hua."

Life he had awarded, it was his
right to take away, but right it wasn't.

Ghalib sat down, quietly. Kalloo came with a glass of sherbet and some dry fruits on a plate. Mufti Saheb pushed the glass towards him. Ghalib leaned back against the wall, his eyes shut. "Mirza? Mirza?" Mufti nudged him.

Ghalib opened his eyes, straightened himself and walked up the stairs to his room. He looked down at the vacant courtyard from the balcony.

Moments of earlier events crossed borders into a sorrowful terrain—the wife of his friend Bansidhar singing, with him standing outside the curtain and Wafadar carrying the child.

He thought of something and then again climbed down the stairs, and went out.

2

The evening was brimming with the blood from the vanity of the swollen sun. Ghalib stood at the fresh grave of his child. A large stone was placed behind the grave. Mirza sat quietly, staring blankly at it. His soul seemed to be engaged in a conversation with his son and he seemed to address him thus:

"Lazim tha ke dekho mera rasta koi din aur
Tanha gay kyun? ab raho tanha koi din aur."

Wise it would have been to wait for me a few days more.
Why did you leave alone? Now be a loner a few days more.

"Jate huay kehte ho, qayamat ko milenge
Kya Khoob! qayamat ka hai goya koi din aur."

'We will meet on Doomsday, you said at parting,
Did you think Doomsday could be any other day than this one.

"Tum kuan se the aise khary dad-satd ke
Karta mulkul-maut taqaza koi din aur."

You were not such a fanatic about business transactions.
Why then didn't you ask death to wait a few days more?

"Asad!" Bansidhar's voice interrupted Ghalib's train of thoughts. "Where are you lost, Asad?"

"I'm thinking," Ghalib said, "of going to the *dargah*."

"To the *dargah!*" Bansidhar looked up in surprise.

"Yes!" Ghalib affirmed. "I'm yet to offer one more *chaddar*. I had offered one when I had wished for a child. I had one more to offer as thanksgiving... now I must offer one as an apology. I troubled him pointlessly..."

Bansidhar placed his hand on his shoulder and with anguish added, "Do not be bitter, Asad."

"I'm not bitter, Lala," Ghalib's voice was choked, "but what should I do with that woman, who is dying slowly of childbirth. She wants to be a mother, but her lap's filled with corpses instead. This was her fifth child, Lala..." Tears welled up in Ghalib's eyes.

"Come, let's go home," Bansidhar took hold of Ghalib by the shoulder and led him away. The sun had sunk into the horizon and was turning its edges behind them.

3

Ghalib sat alone in his room, reclining against a *diwan* propelled by his writing desk, a pen in his hand. A half burnt candle illuminated the room. There was a glass half full of whisky placed within his reach, a bottle half consumed quite near it. A few more bottles, drained of their contents crowded the corner. Some couplets, randomly written, filled a few sheafs:

"Bas ke dushwar hai har kaam ka aasan hona
Admi ko bhi mayasser nahin, insaan hona."

It is indeed difficult for all work to be easy,
It is not easy for man to be a human either.

"Ghar humara, jo na rote bhi tho viraan hota
Behr gar beh, na hota to biyabaan hota."

My house, even if I had not wept would have been desolate,
The sea, if it was not to be, a jungle it would have been.

"Ishrat-e qatra hai darya mein fana ho jana
Dard ka hud se guzarna hai dawa ho jana."

The glory of a droplet is to get assimilated into the river,
The remedy of pain is to cross the borders of endurance.

"Dard minnat kash-e dawa na hua
Main na achha hua, bura na hua."

Pain did not feel grateful to its remedy
And though I was not cured I did feel better.

Another night coursed through the firmament. The only change in the room was in the number of empty bottles in the corner. Ghalib was still engaged in his writing.

"Ibn-e Maryam hua kare koi
Mere dukh ki dawa kare koi."

The son of Mary used to once,
Will someone heal my wounds now.

"Bak raha hoon junoon mein kya kya kuch
Kuch na samjhe khuda kare koi."

What all have I said in this feverish craziness.
May God will it to be incomprehensible.

The crowd of bottles in the corner slowly surged forward near Ghalib's desk.

"Kalloo Miyan!" Ghalib asked him, "have these bottles removed from here. I do not like not their empty faces."

"There is no more whisky left, *huzoor!*" Kalloo said.

"Upturn the bottles for a few drops..."

"Do the bottles dare to withhold a droplet when you drink, Sir?" Kalloo answered.

"Maye se gharaz nishat hai kis ru siya ko
Ik gona be khudi mujhe din raat chahiye."

I seek no pleasure from wine, and be sinner.
A bit of indulgence I do seek day and night.

4

Har Gopal Tufta knocked at Ghalib's terrace room. Ghalib summoned him as soon as he spotted him.

"Have a drink," he offered.

"No, I don't drink," Tufta answerd.

"Not even in winters? It is quite necessary in the cold. There is nothing within to fight the chill otherwise," Ghalib said. Tufta was quite embarrassed.

"Anyway, what brings you here?"

"Ustad," Tufta asked, "do you know anyone named MacPherson?"

"An Englishman. He has a wine shop at Meerut. And another in Dilli. Whatever I need, comes from his shop," Ghalib answered.

"What sort of needs?"

"What do you get at wine shops? Certainly not charcoal for your ovens, Har Gopal," he commented.

"And how come you bought things on credit from this Englishman?

"Because my pension is due on the English."

"But your dues are on the king emperor of India," Tufta said.

"Abu Zaffar may be the king emperor... but God knows who holds the reins. The ruler is Emperor Abu Zafar, but the reins are in the hands of Charles Metcalfe, and the sovereignity is of the British Crown... but tell me, what's the matter?"

"This man MacPherson too has initiated proceedings against you."

"He too? What do you mean by that? Is there someone else besides him?"

"Don't you know, Ustad? Both Mathuradas and Sukhchain have filed suits in the courts against you. They have got the news of your failure at Calcutta."

"Darbarimal's the only one left," Ghalib added after a pause, "let it be known to him too."

"Do you find it amusing? These people are bringing decrees against you and you seem to be unruffled."

Ghalib was unperturbed, "The decrees are not brought against me but against my pension. They trusted me on that hope. My position was that of the witness, Allah's status was of the pension."

Har Gopal kept quiet, unable to refute Ghalib's rhetoric. Kalloo entered almost immediately, unaware of Har Gopal's presence. He stood at the door unable to decide if he should let Mirza know of his errand.

"Yes, Kalloo, there's a decree on your face, say whose case is it now," Ghalib goaded him.

"I'll come again," Kalloo hesitated, "pardon me for interrupting."

"Say it, Kalloo Miyan," Ghalib added, "there's nothing to hide from Tufta."

"Yusuf *bhai*'s Begum and children want to go to Jaipur," Kalloo said hesitantly.

"But why?"

"Perhaps Begum's a bit annoyed and angry. Wants to go to her father's."

Ghalib paused for a moment and then said, "Tell her that arrangements will be made in the morning."

"Yes, Sir!" Kalloo said and left.

"What are you doing?" Tufta turned to him, "tell her, make her understand..."

"Tufta *bhai*," Ghalib sighed, "I myself get tired taking care of Yusuf, what must be falling on that woman. A trip to her father's will do her good. The only wrong is..." he lapsed into a silence.

"What?" Tufta asked.

"Whom shall I seek a loan from now? Darbarimal?"

5

"My pension has been denied at Calcutta, Darbarimal," Ghalib sat at his shop talking to him. "Mathuradas and Sukhchain are bringing decrees against me. But what must I do to my needs, that come on my threshold without fail? Yusuf Miyan's wife and children have to be sent to Jaipur and then my personal needs, you know. Today's wine is due. But for hope, I have nothing to sell or mortgage. My income's a hundred and sixty-two rupees and expenditure rupees three hundred, that is a loss of a hunded and forty rupees per month. You tell me, can you manage in that amount?"

Darbarimal sat chewing a paan and offered him one, saying, "You don't take paan. I have heard you think it to be poison."

"I would have taken it, had it been poison. I do not, because it's paan."

Darbarimal took out his credit ledger and logging an entry said, "I do not know, Mirza why I loan you money, but here I am doing it."

6

"*Adaab,* Mir Saheb!" Mufti Miyan greeted Mir Saheb as he entered his shop.

"*Adaab, adaab!* Greatness be to Allah that you've graced my shop," Mir Saheb said.

"Mir Saheb, I have been looking for Mirza Nausha," Mufti revealed the purpose of his visit.

"He's inside," he said.

Ghalib called, "Come in, Mufti saheb! Greetings!"

"*Adaab,* Mirza Nausha. Now old age has caught up with you too. Greyness peeps out of your beard."

"Rau mein hai rakhsh-e umra kahan dekhiye thhame
Na hath bag par hai, na paa hai rakab mein."

Where does the age horse in full gallop, stop.
Neither the hands are on the rein nor the feet in stirrups.

Mirza recited the couplet with flourish and added as soon as Mufti had settled down. "For what sin and crime am I being hunted down now?"

"I had gone to your house last evening but I learnt that you were engrossed in your drink—that's why I didn't come up."

"You should have, Mufti Saheb! Shared a drink or two with me."

"In this matter, I am Zauq's follower:

"Aye Zauq! dukhtare riz ko na mounh laga
Chutti nahin hai mounh se, yeh kafir lagi hui."

O Zauq do not be so familiar with this lady wine,
It does not leave you, once familiar.

"But why are you so against wine, Sir? What's wrong in drinking?"

"The first and foremost thing is, Mirza, that an alcoholic's prayers are never granted."

"Hear him," Ghalib cut in immediately, "what else would one pray for, when one gets wine?"

They both laughed heartily and soon Mir Saheb appeared with two bowls of qahwa. "There was no need for the formality," both Mufti Saheb and Mirza said.

"Let it be, Sirs," Mir saheb said. "The sun and the moon have themselves graced a poor household. When do such occasions arise so often and then the qahwa is from Palti Darwazaa. It is quite popular."

"Thank you, Mir Saheb, for your kind hospitality," Mirza said and no sooner had he left that he turned to Mufti and asked, "What brings you here, Sir?"

"I have a letter from Hazrat Naasikh Miyan," he flashed a letter from his pocket and explained further. "He writes that there's glory in Deccan these days. Maharaja Chandulal of Hyderabad is a wonderful patron of arts. If you go there, you will wash your hands off poverty..." he paused.

"Firstly, Mufti saheb, it is difficult for me to leave Dilli without paying my debts," Mirza replied, "and then what honour would poor Chandulal bestow on me? Where Qateel is regarded as a master of Persian and Shah Nasir in Urdu, who will honour Ghalib and Naasikh there? Furthermore, Mufti Saheb, that old man is now in his eighties. His feet are already in the grave. By the time I reach Hyderabad, he would have reached the Heavens." They sipped their tea in silence. After a while, Ghalib said, "Let's go, Mufti Saheb,"

"Read this letter from Nashikh Miya!" Mufti said offering him the letter.

"What more will I learn, Mufti Saheb? You did explain things to me. Mir Saheb, we'll take your leave." They both bid adieu to the bookseller and left.

"You did not agree to teach Persian at the Delhi college either, and came back annoyed," Mufti said to Ghalib as they walked down the street.

"Whoever told you this?" Ghalib looked up.

"James Thomson himself! He said that he had three names submitted to him of people in Delhi who are masters in Persian," Mufti said.

"Who were number two and three?" Ghalib asked in his peculiar fashion.

"Hakim Momin Khan Momin and Sheikh Imam Baksh Sahbai."

"Then Thomson must have told you why I refused to take up the job,"

"Yes, he did. That you had come to his door in a palanquin and there was no one at the door to greet you. That's why you returned saying..."

"I was willing to take up work, to enhance my prestige, not to lessen what I have now," Ghalib added spontaneously.

"But you had gone to seek employment..."

"Not as an employee," Ghalib cut in sharply, "but as a scholar of Persian—and at his house, not at the college, not at the school."

A few palanquin bearers passed by. Ghalib, his face flushed in anger, halted one of them. "Mufti saheb," he said, "I know that you were the one who had recommended my name to Thomson Saheb, for you are a friend and a well-wisher and I am a needy man at present; but I have no desire to be sold." He sat in the palanquin and at his bidding the bearers moved on. "*Khuda Hafiz!*" Ghalib wished Mufti Saheb and left him standing where he was. He watched him go and said to himself, "Mirza, you had come to know that the recommendation was mine. You did not wish to take a favour."

7

"You will not accept any employment, your pension will not be awarded, your expenses will not come down, what will you do?" Hiralal chided a subdued Ghalib. "How will you manage? By gambling a lifetime? Forget that the king emperor will ever call you to the fort, not as long as Ibrahim Zauq is the poet laureate."

Ghalib for once kept silent. Hiralal went on, "You have borrowed whatever money you could. In fact, borrowed more than you should have. How will you repay all that? You've nothing to sell or mortgge. The house you live in is rented..." he lapsed into silence and neared Mirza who was strolling restlessly, "I don't know what to do."

"All that you are telling me," Ghalib replied calmly, "I am already aware of. What I do not know is what will happen when Mathuradas will come with the decree tomorrow."

"A few men from the court will come and escort you there," Hiralal replied helplessly.

"Will they also handcuff me?"

"No, they do not have that right, but two policemen will flank you from the back, two at the back. You will cross your lane, your eyes downcast and thus you will reach the court and made to stand in the enclosure."

Ghalib visualised himself, being taken through the *gali,* and that did happen, when Tufta was watching.

8

Ghalib stood in the docks in the court. A magistrate sat at the judge's desk flanked by his officials. Even Tufta was seen in the premises.

Hiralal bowed before him and handed over a few papers to the clerk who passed them on to the presiding magistrate. Hiralal touched Ghalib's hands and walked by.

Ghalib stood buried in his own thoughts, "I've been reduced to a spectator of my own humiliation. I talk to myself and say here's one more nail in your coffin, you did take pride in your own self, weren't you too vain about being a great poet and thought that there was no parallel to your grasp of Persian. Now answer your creditors—say something, speak. But what do you have to say? Shameless, no self-respect. You took stuff from the vittner, the perfume-maker, the cloth merchant, the fruit merchants, the moneylenders. Did you ever think of repaying them and where from?"

fourteen

I

"KEEP SOME ***SHAMMI KABABS*** too, Wafadar—they are his favourite," Umrao was instructing her. She was not that young now and her hair had greyed at the temples. "He must be feeling really hungry at the gaol. Nothing to do but lie down all day," Umrao Begum added.

"Kalloo Miyan said that he keeps either reading or writing the entire day in the gaol." Wafadar said. "Nawab Shefta comes over every second day to pay a visit."

"They don't give him wine, do they?" Umrao Jaan said with eagerness, as if she wished they did give him his wine and then realized that they didn't. She came out into the courtyard, where 'Lalain' was sitting on a *charpai* chopping vegetables. Age showed on her too. Umrao tried to take the chopping knife from Lalain in an effort to relieve her from the job.

"Let it be, Umrao," she said, "I will do it." Umrao sat down quietly. Her eyes brimmed with tears and she started to cry.

"Have patience, Umrao," there was sympathy in Lalain's voice, "and don't you cry all day."

"I had an intution the day he befriended those rich brats," she complained.

"Whom are you talking about?" Lalain asked

"The sons of jewellers of the Chandini Chowk. They would sit there in his room gambling all day and all night. I had asked him once..."

"Who is gambling?" Ghalib stood near the door rebuking Begum, "and if they stake the bets, why must I withdraw?"

"It was a different story when Mirza Khani was the Kotwal, but this new officer, Faizal Hasan seems to be your sworn enemy. God forbid someday..."

"He will not," Ghalib snubbed Umrao. "Has God ever done any thing you had asked Him for. I am aware of your rapport with God."

"And the very next day," she wiped her tears, "I was in the *baithak* inside, when they raided the house. The Kotwal went straight up to the room along with his men."

Wafadar came running.

"Begum! Begum Sahiba, *huzoor's* topi and cloak, they are taking him to the kotwali," Wafadaar gushed in.

"Kotwali? Why kotwali? Who are these people?" Umrao asked.

"The Kotwal perhaps. These people were gambling. The kotwal caught them red-handed. And he accused *huzoor* of running a gambling den and thus asked him too to come to the kotwali."

"*Allah!*" Umrao could merely gasp and slouched down. Wafadar rushed out with Ghalib's topi and cloak.

Umrao had begun to cry again, bitterly.

"You need not worry, Umrao," Bansidhar's wife said, "he has gone there, hasn't he. He will try and have him acquitted and if need be, he will even go to the fort."

2

"Hand this letter to Magistrate Wazir Ali Khan," Bahadur Shah Zafar summoned one of his aides, "and let it be known to him that it is our personal wish that Mirza Nausha be acquitted without any punishment."

The aide took the letter.

Zafar added, "We shall personally plead his case to the present resident."

The moment the aide left, an attendant announced, "*Zilae Subhani*, Maulana Nasiruddin seeks your permission to present himself before you."

"Bid him enter, Kale Miyan is our pir, our guru." A middle aged fakir entered the hall, dressed in a black robe, a rosary in his right hand.

"Allah! Allah!" he blessed the king emperor and then said, "I have heard that you are a bit worried about Mirza Nausha!"

"Yes, Sir, I am. The city Kotwal has him locked in prison—under the anti-gambling act. He is a fine poet, Kale Miyan, but the vices of wine and gambling have him in their grip."

"His pleasures are quite royal, his means meager, thus his ill-repute. One of your couplets suits him best:"

"Yaa mujhe afsar shahana banaya hota
Yaa mera taj gad yana banaya hota.

Either I would have been an officer royal,
or my crown still over my head.

Khaksaari ke liy gar-cha banaya tha mujhe
Kash khak-e dare janana banaya hota."

If you had to make me in dust
you should have made me the dust of your doorstep.

Zafar recited the next couplet.

"If I could have, Pir Saheb," Zafar added, "I would have placed him in court, to be near me but what must I do? First, the court is no longer what it used to be and secondly, I find myself helpless as long as Zauq is there."

"But you must find a way to save him from disgrace," Kale Miyan said. "Devise a way to provide him with an income,"

"Ghalib will not accept any designation lesser than of poet laureate—a second position he will not agree to."

"He is a scholar of Persian. Engage him to write the history of the Taimuria Dynasty. His class and respect will not be lessened thus," Kale Khan advised. Zafar kept quiet. Kale Mian further added, "All of Dilli today echoes with the news of Ghalib's imprisonment. Tell me, is that kind of treatment to be meted out to a ordinary gambler or a great poet?"

3

Ghalib sat confined within his cell, gathering his thoughts in a bunch of verses. His thoughts rattled on in the darkness of the night and he intoned the verses as they came to him:

"Dost gham khuwari mein meri sayi farmaenge kya
Zakhm ke bharne talak, nakhun na barh aenge kya."

What can friends do to mitigate my pain,
when the wounds heal, will not the nails be longer.

"Hazrate naseh gar ayen deeda-O-dil farsh-e rah:
Koi mujh ko ye tho samjha do ke samjhaenge kya."

The heart and the soul lie at service for the preacher,
but what is he to say, must not someone tell me?

4

There was jubilation at Zauq's place, untouched by the serenity that prevailed in Ghalib's cell in jail. Zauq sat surrounded by his disciples. Age had not spared them either; the crowd had a few youngsters—Zauq's new disciples.

"I knew," Zauq said, "the fate that meets a clever crow."

"The brick has settled where it belong. Isn't that so Yaas Miyan?" one said.

"You unnecessarily worried yourself, Sir," another addressed Zauq.

"I do regret," Zauq said by way of explanation, "Mirza Ghalib's humiliation at the hands of Miyan Kotwal but more than that, I regret the fact that King Emperor Zafar had to plead before a mere *firangi* for a small-time gambler—and that too for a plea rejected. Even the Munsif Magistrate showed no regard for him and awarded Mirza six months rigorous imprisonment and a fine of two hundred rupees." The gathering regretted the fact along with Zauq, though in their heart of hearts, they knew that Zauq enjoyed every bit of it.

5

Ghalib was engrossed in his writing.....

"Gar kya naseh ne hum ko qaid, achha yu'n sahi
Ye janune ishq ke andaz chhutt jaenge kya.

What if the preacher holds me capture
This craziness of love, must it desert me.

Khana zad-e zulf hain, zanjir se bhagen ge kyun
Hain girftaar-e wafa, zanda'n se ghabraenge kya.

Tied in love-lock that I am, must
I run away from prison.

Hai ab ees mamure mein qaht-e gham-e ulfat Asad
Hum ne ye mana keh Dilli mein rahen, khaenge kya."

There's dearth in this city, of pangs of unrequited love,
And though I am agreed to stay in Dilli, what must I feed myself on.

6

When Kotwal Faizul Hassan entered the kotwali, Hakim Momin was waiting for him. Momin asked for permission to enter. The Kotwal said, "Please do come. Have a seat. I am sure you have come for that prisoner."

"Yes. I have come to meet him. I am also carrying a letter for you."

"Whose recommendation have you brought this time?"

Laughing, Hakim Momin replied, "Doctor Raas. He had accompanied Nawab Shefta the last time."

The Kotwal expressed his compulsion. "Let me make two things very clear, Hakim Momin saheb. Firstly, his release is not in my hand, albeit his arrest was, for gambling, which is a crime punishable by law. And to arrest the criminal is my duty. But his release...that can only come from the court."

Hakim Momin nodded his head in agreement and said, "And the second thing?"

"Secondly, he had been awarded rigorous imprisonment for six months. Even though the emperor had pushed his case, we could not release him. Nonetheless, his confinement was made lenient. His food and clothing is sent from home. His friends and well wishers come and meet him without any difficulty; only the time is an issue. What other comforts can a prisoner expect?"

Momin said, "Whatever you might say, imprisonment *is* imprisonment, after all."

The Kotwal turned to look sharply at Momin."Really? Why does Nawab Shefta have such an attachment with a gambler and drunkard? This is not becoming of him."

"Look here, Kotwal saheb. Ghalib has never made any claims to piousness. Nawab saheb's devotion towards Ghalib is due to his creative capabilities. He is one of the greatest poets of this period. He is no less a poet if he drinks or gambles!" After a moment of silence, Momin added, "And where this association is concerned, history will make mention of both of you, because in one way or the other, you are both linked to Ghalib!" At this, he handed over Doctor Raas' letter to the Kotwal who nearly snatched it away. "If history begins to make mention of gamblers..." He left his sentence incomplete and started to read the letter.

Momin said, "Doctor Raas has submitted a petition to the court saying that Ghalib's health takes a turn for the worse in prison. There is another letter addressed to you requesting your consent."

The Kotwal turned towards Momin in anger and said,"Why do you want to make me a party to your lies? What discomfort is he facing? He is in absolutely good health and stays in good spirits. I regret the fact that I have never seen him under the weather!"

Momin looked completely taken aback at this.

7

Ghalib looked in good spirits. There weren't any signs of worry or displeasure on his face. He seemed deeply engrossed in a book sitting in his cell. He suddenly heard the soft crying of somebody close by. He shut his book and looked around to try and make out where the sound was coming from. A guard on duty passed outside his cell and he called out to him,"Come here a moment." The guard went happily towards

Ghalib's cell, the door of which was open. The guard stepped inside and said, "Yes, Sir?"

Ghalib asked him with deep concern, "Who is crying? I have been hearing him since the morning."

The guard replied, "It is a young boy, Sir. He has been arrested for some crime and has been imprisoned for a period of three months. He has been awarded solitary confinement."

"Oh," Ghalib replied, "so he is unable to bear the loneliness."

"Yes," the guard nodded in agreement.

"Okay, you may leave."

A little hesitatingly the guard said, "May I present a couplet to you?"

Ghalib turned to him in anger and said, "This is not the time to recite couplets. Go!"

At this the guard beat a hasty retreat and left the cell. Ghalib sat down with his book once again and had barely turned a page when he heard the crying once more. He got up, steadied himself with his walking stick and stepped out of his cell into the corridor.

Ghalib reached the prisoner's cell and addressed him from the other side. "What is the matter?"

In between his sobs, the boy replied, "I have been imprisoned for three months."

"So what is there to cry about?" Ghalib asked.

"I was to get married today," the boy replied.

Ghalib smiled and said, "You should think yourself to be lucky! You are saved from serving a life sentence! God is kind. You should thank the Kotwal that he has done one more good deed and saved you from getting married. This prison sentence will get over, but the imprisonment of marriage never will!"

At this the boy stopped crying and looked at Ghalib, who had already turned around and was walking back to his cell.

8

"Begum Sahiba!" Wafadar's voice traced Umrao and Mirza's terrace room where she was busy dusting and arranging his books. Wafadar followed soon after.

"What's it, Wafadar?" Umrao asked

"Haji Mir has come. Wants to talk to you."

"I shall be down in a moment."

"Why don't you call him up here and speak with him from behind the curtain?" Wafadar advised.

Umrao nodded. Wafadar called from the terrace, "Do come up on the terrace, Mir Saheb."

A visibly aged Haji Mir travelled up the stairs. Wafadar dropped the curtain for Begum to stand behind.

"Greetings, Begum Sahiba," Haji Saheb paid his respects and said, "I am known as Haji Mir, Begum Sahiba, and have a small bookshop."

As soon as Haji Mir was through with introduction, Umrao said, "I know you, Mir Saheb. Doesn't Mirza spend his entire day at your bookshop? He has much praise for you, Sir,"

"Oh! I do not merit the praises," Haji Saheb touched his forehead. "I had come to let you know that Mirza Nausha's *diwan* that had been calligraphed at Agra and had been lying with me, has gone to press for publication. A little advance that I could gather is here at your service. Perhaps you may need it."

"Thank you, Haji saheb!" Umrao heaved a sigh of relief both for the publication and the money in these hard times. "May Allah grant you your wishes." She then turned towards Wafadar and said, "Take the money from Haji saheb," and turning to Haji Mir said, "he is not home since the last three months, you must be aware of that."

"I do. Nawab Shefta has gone to meet the resident with recommendations from a civil surgeon in Delhi. Perhaps he will be released in a couple of days."

"May God will it to be so. He may do whatsoever he feels like once is back," she just muttered.

"I will take your leave now but do let me know if I can be of any service to you," Haji turned to go.

Umrao turned to Wafadar, "Go get some purchases from the grocer's—and where is Kalloo Miyan?"

"Went to the washerman, but hasn't returned as yet," Wafadaar replied.

Umrao busied herself once again in cleaning Mirza's room. Finally, she removed his clothes from the pegs and climbed down the stairs. The outer door to the house was open. She shut it and stepped back into the courtyard and was shocked to find Mirza sitting on the *diwan* with his head bowed, a walking stick in his hand. For the first time, Umrao noticed the whiteness of his beard. How finely had age painted them. She stood there, watching him, holding her breath. Tears suddenly welled up in her eyes. She sat down behind him, leaned against his back, her head on his shoulder and cried. Mirza's eyes were vacant and lost.

fifteen

I

"THE WORST WORRY was," Mirza sat narrating his jail experiences at Tufta's house surrounded by friends, relishing mangoes, "the passing away of the mango-season during my jail-term." They all laughed. Mirza continued, "My sins would have been forgiven at the Lord's, but the magistrate, I would have never forgiven him for this inconsideration."

"Shall I have something else sent?" Tufta's Begum asked from behind the veil.

"There's no need for anything else, sister," Ghalib said, "as long as there are enough mangoes."

"But," Nawab Shefta led the conversation back on track, "the magistrate did favour you in a way. Your term was six months' rigorous imprisonment, the magistrate spared you the rigour."

"Not for the first month," Ghalib chipped in, "five lashes a day did I receive, without fail."

"Lashes?" Everyone was surprised and looked at each other. Ghalib peacefully sucked at the mango.

"But you being lashed—that's impossible, Mirza!" Shefta remarked.

"A policeman, Sir," Ghalib explained, "assigned the job to watch over me turned out to be a little poetic. Everyday he would read out five couplets of his and would wait for appreciation. Every couplet was equivalent to a lash and he skinned me off in a month."

They all laughed again. "But how did you free yourself of him?" Tufta asked.

"With great difficulty did I ask the *daroga* to have him transferred," Ghalib revealed.

"Mirza Nausha," Tufta pointed out a young man amongst them. "I would like to introduce this young man, he writes good verses and desires to be your disciple."

The mango slipped away from Ghalib's hands and he exclaimed, "Rigorous? How many more couplets now?" The young man blushed and the others laughed.

"I'm a great admirer of yours, Sir," the man added, "and come from far away. Do not disappoint me with your refusal, Sir."

"Where have you come from?" Ghalib was impressed by the sincerity in his voice,

"From Panipat, Sir,"

"What's your name?"

"Altaaf Hussain."

"And your nom de plume?"

"Hali."

"Hali," Ghalib nodded, "Good! It is accepted."

The man went down on his knees and kissed Ghalib's soiled hands and touched them to his forehead. With the passage of time, Hali came to be known as Mirza Ghalib's most dear and faithful disciple.

2

"Najmuddaullah, Dabirumulk, Nizam-e-Jung Mirza Asadullah Khan Ghalib, we welcome you in this our royal court."

On the fourth day of July 1850, Bahadur Shah Zafar received Mirza Ghalib in his court thus in the presence of Zauq, Kale Miyan, Mufti and many others. Ghalib was presented a royal robe, a shawl, jewels and gold coins on a silver platter which he accepted and handed over to an attendant. Zafar, the king emperor personally presented him a garland and a green sash. People stood up in reverence and congratulated him. Kale Miyan touched him with his rosary.

Mufti Sadaruddin embraced him.

3

"Be happy, Begum," Ghalib nudged his wife, "your wishes have been granted."

"But he only presented you the titles—Dainumulk, Naginu..."

"Uh-hoon! Najmudaullah, Dabirumulk, Nizam-e-Jung..." Ghalib corrected.

"But they are all titles. Did he give you any cash?"

"Yes, the gold coins and the jewels and an assignment to write down the history of the Taimur Dynasty. And when he's given me that responsibility, the fee too would be something of Taimur's befitting."

"What if he doesn't'?"

"I'll alter the history," Ghalib added with a smile. "I'll do what Firdausi did to Mahmud Ghazni while writing his biography. If one tries to take liberties with a poet, that's inevitable." His wife handed him a glass of wine. "He may be the king of the scepter," he continued, "I'm the emperor of the pen. His kingdom may be snatched from him, my domain none can take away from me," he got up and walked towards the door. "I'll go pay Mirza Yusuf a visit," and he went away.

4

Mirza Yusuf sat playing with a mouse. He had the mouse's tail tied with a thread on a spool and would pull it towards him and then leave it to run away. An attendant hovered around him trying to feed him his food. Yusuf remained oblivious to Ghalib's entry. "Kalyan!" Ghalib asked the servant, "what's all this affair?"

"*Huzoor!*" Kalyan's condition was pathetic, "he doesn't eat if we do not amuse him with antics." Ghalib came near Yusuf, wiped his soiled face and asked politely, "Yusuf Miyan, shall I have your children and wife called from Jaipur?"

Yusuf Miyan shook his head.

"Do you ever think about your children?"

He shook his head again.

"How does he feel now?" Ghalib asked Kalloo.

"Hakim Saheb does come to monitor his health but to no avail," Kalyan answered. Yusuf Miyan ran out with the mouse.

Ghalib called after him, "Yusuf!"

But he did not come back. Ghalib turned to Kalyan, "Do not let him go out, I worry about him, Kalyan. I would have kept him with me but I have called Aarif's children, Wakar and Hussain over. Now they are to stay with me." He thrust some money in Kalyan's hands, "Keep this, you may need it."

Hali rushed in and impatiently blurted, "I'd been to your house, *huzoor*, and learnt that you would be here..."

"Why, what's the matter?" Ghalib enquired.

"Some sad news, huzoor!"

Ghalib paused and then asked, "Why, what has happened?

"Ustaad Zauq has passed away."

"*Innalillah wa Inna Illae Rajeon,*" Ghalib uttered a prayer.

5

Zauq's funerel passed through the bazaar.

Laie hayat, aae, qaza le chali chale
Apni khushi na aae, na apni khushi chale.

Life brought me here, death takes me away
It wasn't my will to come, it's not my will to go.

Ghalib joined Zauq's funeral.

6

The street was completely blocked by the cots and *charpais* and *moorahs* on which Ghalib and his friends relaxed. A basket of ripe mangoes was in attendence next to them.

"*Arrey bhai*, Hakim Saheb," Ghalib coaxed Hakim Raziuddin, "taste at least one, please."

"No thanks," Hakim replied, "I do not eat mangoes. I'm happy with my sherbet."

"Your anthology," Haji Mir addressed Ghalib, "has been pretty readily accepted, Mirza Saheb, and I believe a second edition is underway in Lucknow."

"Nawab Wajid Ali Shah, it is heard, is getting it weighed against gold coins," another said.

"That's a good act on his part," Ghalib quipped. "but it would be better if after having it weighed, he keeps the anthology and has the coins sent to me." There was laughter all around.

"Mufti Saheb," someone said, "you've well toned your hair with mango juice."

"Age hasn't touched you, Mufti Saheb," Ghalib added. "Your hair is as white as it was in your adolescence. Hasn't blackened with age."

They all laughed. Even Mufti joined in the laughter.

"Mirza *bhai*," Mufti saheb asked, "please write that plea for me which you read before the king emperor yesterday."

"What was it, let us hear," Haji too pleaded.

"Hardly anything, Haji Saheb," Ghalilb said, "it is a custom at the fort to pay the courtiers biannually—that is to say that even I would get paid twice a year. What would I have done to pay for my daily needs—fall in the same trap of the money lenders and it's misery. So I pleaded to the emperor."

"*Bhai*," Mufti tried to impress upon the assembly, "he pleaded to the king emperor then and there in verse. I did not have a chance to write it down."

"What did you say," the others requested, "let us hear it too."

"I do not remember all the verses," Ghalib said, "but it went something like this:

'Aey Shahensha-e aasma aurang
aey jahandar aftab aasar!
Bare naukar bhi ho gaya sad shukr
nisbatein hogein mushkhus char.'

O! King of the sky and the earth
O! Ye sun of the entire universe.

I cannot recall anything further."

"You skipped that verse," Mufti said, "It is the dead that have their rites once per six months. And that's a rite they stick to."

Ghalib caught up with the lines that followed:
Look at me, pulsating with life I am.
And six-monthly means only twice a year.
I haven't bought a thing this year
I haven't built a thing this time.
Fire by the night and the sunshine by the day

To hell with such comforts
I've to seek loans every month.
And the money-lenders seek their interests.
So much so that one-third of my salary befalls the share of the money-lender.
I be your man and run in the buff
Your servant and feed on loans.
Grant me my wages every month so life does not prove to be a burden.

"Tum salamat raho hazar baras
har baras ke hon din pachas hazaar."

May you live a thousand years,
And may there be fifty thousand days to every year.

Everyone burst into an applause.

"The king emperor," Mufti added, "granted him his plea then and there."

Just then a donkey strolled into the lane pulling a cart followed by its master.

"Bhai jaan," Hali said, "it will be kind of you to take the other lane, why must you make all of us get up?"

The donkey sniffed at a mango-skin and trotted away, refusing to eat it.

"Mirza," Hakim Saheb caught on to the opportunity, "did you notice? The donkey merely sniffed the mango-skin and left it. Mangoes—even the asses do not eat."

"Yes, Sir," Ghalib retorted, "asses don't eat mangoes."

The gathering once again burst into laughter. Before the laughter could subside, Shams arrived on horseback from the other side. He seemed to be agitated. He dismounted his horse and approached Ghalib who got up to receive him.

"Come hither, Shams bhai," Ghalib said

"Greetings, Sir!" Shams addressed Ghalib's peers and then turned towards him, "how are you, Asad bhai?" He took his seat next to him.

"What brings you here?" Ghalib asked.

"Your reach now extends to the royal court, Asad Bhai," Shams said, "ask the king emperor to do something about our pension."

"That affair is not in his hands, Shams," Ghalib answered.

"Ask him to talk to the resident," Shams pleaded, "the whole affair rests in the hands of William Frazer. If he so wishes, our case can be decided in a day."

"Look here, Shams," Ghalib was irritated, "on your insistence earlier, I went all the way to Calcutta, in vain. I do not intend to raise that issue all over again. But if I can do something, be of help financially, I am willing..."

Shams was quiet for a moment, then got up abruptly and left saying, "I'll meet this Frazer alright, all by myself. *Khuda Hafiz!*" They all watched him mount his horse and desperately gallop away.

sixteen

I

GHALIB SAT ON his *diwan* writing letters against the flickering flame. A few letters and envelopes were stacked against his writing-desk and Kalloo Miyan sat sealing a few others. His glass of whisky, wrapped in red muslin, rested atop the desk.

"Listen, Kalloo Miyan," Mirza stopped midway and said, "this letter to Mundi, Jawahar Singh Jauhari, you must post first thing in the morning. The rest you may do so tomorrow evening when the envelopes are ready. I've the paper for the envelopes cut to size. Tomorrow we'll both sit down and have them glued."

"Yes, Sir," Kalloo Miyạn said.

Ghalib once again lost himself in his letter.

"I do not need a cap," he wrote, "but I do want a silken lungi, like the ones made in Peshawar and Multan, but one which is not gaudy or brightly coloured, the borders not too loud, the embroidery must be delicate and pleasing but not with threads of gold or silver. Look for silk that's black or green or khaki and pale and on completion have it sent by post and tell me the cost too. If you do not do so, I shall not accept it. Do not delay sending the lungi and do not be formal in writing its cost."

He paused, read the letter once again, then appended his signature underneath.

2

A troop of four British soldiers passed by Haji Mir's shop followed by two more soldiers and a hand-cuffed man. Haji Mir watched them from his shop. Curiosity brought him to the door. He seemed to have recognized the hand-cuffed man.

"Shams, that was Shams," he said to himself. He craned forward to be sure. "That's Shams alright," he told himself. He went back to his shop wondering what to do, "Shall I tell Mirza?" he asked himself. He toyed with the idea for some time and then said to the neighbouring shopkeeper, "Ayaaz bhai, keep an eye on my shop. I'll just be back." He literally ran. He had hardly gone any distance that he came back and told Ayaaz bhai, "If Mirza Ghalib happens to be here, ask him to wait. I'm going to look for him," he ran towards Mirza's house.

3

"Bibi," Haji Mir caught sight of Mirza's maidservant who had just stepped out of the threshold.

"Greetings, Haji Saheb," Wafadaar recognized the man.

"Greetings! Is Mirza home?" he asked.

"No, Sir! He's not to be found at home. Goes to the fort right in the morning. The king emperor had him summoned. Must be for counsel."

"I do not have any reach to the fort, but he does come for his lunch? Perhaps?" there was still a ray of hope.

"Yes, in the afternoon. The king emperor has had 'besni' roti sent for him. The royal servants themselves had brought it," Wafadaar divulged the information, with pride.

"Tell him..." he was about to say, but decided otherwise, "*khuda hafiz!*" He was plainly disappointed.

4

As he reached his shop he was surprised to see it being closed down. Ayaaz had, in fact, been waiting for him. A strange quietness had spread in the bazaar.

"What's happened, Ayaaz Bhai?" he asked.

"Mir Saheb," Ayaaz said, "these discoloured foreigners are spreading like plague. They are not traders as they profess but seem to be creations of Satan. Eating away the innards of Hindustan, like termites. Have you ever seen the sun being eclipsed? The same thing is happening to Hindustan." He looked around helplessly.

"But tell us, what's happened?" someone from a group standing a little away asked.

"Tell me, is it done?" Ayaaz said, "catch hold of anyone whenever you feel like. Hand-cuff him? Imprison him? Who are these people? I ask, who are they?"

"Who have they arrested now?" Haji Mir asked unable to interpret Ayaaz's ramblings,

"Our Nawab Wajid Ali Shah!" Aayaz's voice was filled with anger and fury, "arrested and deported to Calcutta. Imprisoned there in the Matiya Burj."

"But tell me, who arrested him?" Haji Mir asked as he closed his shop and locked it.

"These Brits, who else, Mir Saheb?"

"No, no, who were the people to actually arrest him, who were those soldiers?" Haji Saheb explained his question.

"The soldiers—Hindustani, who else?"

Haji Saheb looked at him and Ayaaz added, "Were they not ashamed to put their hands on their own Nawab Wajid Ali Shah? Were their souls so coarsened?" In a flash of anger, he picked up a bowl of glass and crashed it on the ground.

5

Mirza sat at Nanbai's shop at Masjid Chowk. The canopies fluttered in the breeze but there was an unusual silence in the air. A few people sat huddled on a bench around Mirza.

"I've heard a Pathan has killed him," one of them declared in a conspiratorial whisper. Ghalib shook his hand in a gesture that spelled 'no' and said with a sigh, "I know who killed William Frazer. It has to be him."

"Who, Mirza Saheb?" one of them asked.

Mirza merely nodded and muttered, "There's one, a Nawab! A robbed and downtrodden Nawab."

He got up and walked towards his home in measured steps leaning on his walking stick. Surdas' bhajan echoes behind him:

"Bisar gai sab taat parai..."

6

Somebody came running behind him. Mirza stopped to see. The man halted and said in between his heavy panting, "Mirza Saheb!" he paused for breath, "*Aadab!* There is some bad news I've brought for you. Mir Saheb asked me to let you know. Nawab Shamsuddin was hanged to death, this morning at the crack of dawn, outside the Kashmiri Gate."

"*Innalillahe...*"

Before Mirza could mouth the prayer, the messenger cautioned, "And for God's sake, do not step outside your threshold, the town's under a riot, there is shooting in the town. Please go home. *Khuda Hafiz!*" And the man ran away. Mirza slowly trudged on, his feet as heavy as lead.

7

Dilli, 1857.

A gun boomed somewhere. Ghalib went home and wrote in his diary: '11 May 1857. Thursday. All directions are filled with the sounds of galloping hooves and scampering feet. After killing the Brits, the rebels camped in the city. They turned the gardens in the Fort into their stables...

'The king emperor could not house such a large contingent nor provide for them, and as a fallout, he was swayed by its power.

'The battle began and canon-balls rained like pellets...' The boom of a canon sounded in the distance.

8

The following night, Ghalib was at his desk writing away furiously, 'When the British contingent entered the city, the people began being slaughtered without relief. The rebels left in the city took them on. And for three days, the area between Kashmiri Gate and Chandini Chowk became a veritable battlefield. All the houses and shops in the city remained bolted. The provisions at houses got over, even water. When it rained, people collected water in bed sheets... After four months and four days did the British establish themselves again over Dilli and their soldiers patrolled the city all nights...'

A distant gun shot could be heard in the room and then a knock at the door. Ghalib picked up his walking stick and peeped into the courtyard. His Begum too had come out of her room and stood in the verandah. Kalloo appeared with a lantern. The knock sounded again at the door. Ghalib stepped down the stairs and asked, "Who is it, Kalloo Miyan?"

"I do not know, Sir," he said, "I'll just find out," and moved towards the door.

"No, wait," Ghalib said, "I too shall come." He crossed the courtyard and opened the door. Kalyan stood framed against the doorway. A Sikh soldier stood beside him.

"Kalyan! You, at this hour of the night, and who's this man with you?" Ghalib asked.

"The soldier of the Maharaja of Patiala," Kalyan answered.

"Raja Narendra Singh?"

"Yes, Sir," the soldier answered and added. "We have brought some bad news for you Ghalib Saheb! Your brother, Yusuf Mirza, his days are over..."

"His days over?" Mirza almost screamed.

"We were all sleeping. God knows when Yusuf Miyan got up and strayed on to the street," Kalyan explained, "a few white soldiers were on patrol. A shot killed him."

Ghalib murmered a prayer.

"The Maharaja has kept us to guard the family of Hakim Sharif Khani," the soldier added. "He said that I should let you know..."

Ghalib looked back at his Begum who stood still on the verandah.

"Let's go, light the way," Ghalib said, his head beamed.

"Ghalib Saheb," the soldier cautioned, "you cannot step outside in the street. The orders are..."

"If I do not step out, who will shroud and bury my brother?" Ghalib said.

"It's very tense and volatile outside, Ghalib Saheb. With great difficulty have I escorted Kalyan. It would be better if you do not venture out," the concerned soldier tried to rationalize.

Ghalib agreed with a heavy heart, "Stay here, I'll be back," He walked through the courtyard and came back with two white bedsheets. He handed them over to Kalyan. Kalloo too joined the Sikh soldier and Kalyan. They stepped into the street. Ghalib picked up the lantern and shut the door. He slowly crossed the courtyard, and thought aloud as he hung the lantern:

"Zulmat kad-a, mein mere, shab gham ka josh hai
Ek shama hai dalil-e sahar, so khamosh hai.

A storm of gloom rages in my dark house
A lovely candle holds the flame, helplessly.

"Ne masuda-e visal, na nazara-e jamal
Mudat hui ke aashti-e chasm-O-gosh hai."

No news of the beloved, no sight of her
No reasons for the eyes and ears to envy another

Daghe firaq sohbat-e shab ki jali hui
Ik shama rah gai hai, so woh bhi khamosh hai."

All that reminds of the night of union is a burnt spot
Even the candle that was the witness is sileut.

"Aate hain ghaib se, ye maza-meen khayal mein
Ghalib! harir khana, nuwae sarosh hai."

These thoughts stray from the sky into my head
Ghalib, the sound of the pen is God's messenger.

seventeen

I

"WHERE ARE YOU OFF to, so early in the morning?" Umrao's voice arrested Ghalib's steps as he was about to step out. The *aazaan* called the faithful to the prayer.

Ghalib stopped with a frown. "Do you always have to question me when I am about to leave? Must you put a watch on me day in and day out?"

"*Aay haay!* I am scared that someone's evil eye may fall on you," Begum was at the door.

"Why? Do you think I'll run away?

"No! You didn't, when there were so many of those kohl-eyed to run away with you."

"Then why do you get up so early in the morning?"

"I do so for my Allah. Look, listen to His call. It's you who do not pay heed to it. You do go to the mosque everyday but why must you retreat your steps?"

"He sends me back, that's why. Had he called me, wouldn't I have been with him by now?"

Umrao was disapproving of the remark.

"'Now you come back early—there is an epidemic in the city. The aftermath of the revolt had barely loosened its clutches on the city, that this plague has taken it into its grip. God knows what the fate of this city will be?"

"What plague? What epidemic? I'm a seventy-one year old man and you a sixty-nine year old woman. Had anyone of us been dead, then would we have known of an epidemic," he trundled on tapping his stick on the street. Begum went back into the courtyard.

Ghalib muttered as he went:

"Rahiye ab aysi jagah chal kar jahan koi na ho
Hum sukhan koi na ho, aur hum zuban koi na ho."

Let us go and reside at a place where there is no one, no one to share your thoughts, or your language.

He turned to look towards his house. Begum was nowhere in sight.

"Pariye gar bimar tho, koi na ho timardar
Aur agar mar jai-e tho, noha khuwan koi na ho."

And if you are to fall sick do so where there is no one to nurse,
And if you are to die, do so where no one to shed tears.

2

Ghalib finished reading his *fateha* on a grave and was walking away when somebody called him from under the banyan tree, "Mirza Nausha?"

A fakir stood under the tree. "Allah...Allah," he blessed Ghalib with his rosary when he neared him.

"Kale Miyan, you here?" Ghalib was surprised

"A fancy has brought me here to sit on this exit door. I take a look at every departing soul." They walked towards the door. Kale Miyan asked, "But what brings you here?"

"I owed Shams a prayer, a *fateha* I came to pay it here, Kale Miyan.

I was grieved to hear your house being vandalised."

"And even your Begum's jewellery," Kale Khan smiled. "She had kept them at my house when she heard of the mutiny."

"The old woman did not let me know it!" Ghalib remarked

"And how are your friends?" Kale Miyan asked.

"Bhai Tufta now has settled down in Meerut. He had a house there earlier. Mufti Sadruddin Saheb has retired to Lahore. Half of Nawab Shefta's belongings and properties been annexed of their estate by the Brits. Only the other day, Hakim Raziuddin had joked that asses do not like mangoes. He fell victim to a Khaki's bullet. The two young sons of Talyar Khan have been hanged. Munshi Hira Lal and Balmukund helped us at the cost of their lives or else only Allah knows what fate would have had in store for the Muslims of Dilli during the Mutiny."

"Now, these separated friends," Kale Khan remarked, "will meet on Doomsday."

"No, not there either," Ghalib observed. "There's going to be flocks divided in sections of Shia, Sunni, the good, the bad,"

"Bhai Mirza," Kale Miyan asked, "I heard you too were summoned by the Whites."

"A few Whites leaped across the wall and entered the gali," Ghalib narrated. "The sepoys of Patiala tried much to hold them but they landed straight at my place. Somebody had informed that I not only had helped the rebels but also sheltered them in my house."

"Then?" Kale Mian goaded.

"What else—they had me and a few others marched to the fort."

"Really?" Kale Miyan asked disbelievingly.

"They were trying to find out where all the Muslims lived in the city. We were all brought to the same place where once we used to meet our king emperor. There was some Colonel Brown at the interrogation. When my turn came, he asked me one single question, 'Asad Ullah Khan Ghalib, are you a Musalmaan?' 'Janab, only half so,' I replied."

'Half! Half Musalmaan. What do you mean by that?' he was surprised.

" 'I drink fermented wine but do not partake of pork meat, that's why I said half,' I justified."

'Good! Good! He can't be a rebel,' he said and suddenly laughed.

3

"That joke made it easy for me but Zafar, he haunted me that day—he was a great king."

"I wonder, Mirza, if you know," Kale Miyan's face suddenly turned serious.

"What?" Ghalib asked

"On Friday, the seventh day of November, King Emperor Zafar left this earth for his heavenly abode. He was buried in Rangoon."

Ghalib gasped as he read a prayer and tears streamed down his face.

4

That night, Masjid Chowk reverberated with Pir Kale Miyan's singing. He lent a soul-rendering voice to Bahadur Shah Zafar's composition:

"Ya mujhe afsar-e shahana banaya hota
Ya mera taj gadyana banaya hota."

Either you should've make me an officer royal
or given me the crown of a fakir.

The voice created magic in the night. People listened to him spellbound, from corners of the streets, from their terraces and balconies. His voice echoed and re-echoed from the monuments of the city and filled every home, every heart.

"Khaksari ke liey garcha banaya tha mujhe
Kaash khak-e dar janana banaya hota."

Made me that you did to kiss dust
Wish you had made me, The dust of beloved's doorstep.

"Nasha-e Isq ka gar zarf diya tha mujh ko
Umer ka tang na paymana banaya hota."

Awarded that you did me with the intoxication of love
Wish you had filled my goblet to the brim.

"Roz mamura-e dunya mein kharabi hai Zafar
Aysi basti ko tho virana banaya hota."

There's something amiss with this world Zafar
Wish this habitation was wilderness.

Ghalib too stood on the balcony of his house, looking into the half lit lonely street.

5

"*Assalaam Walekum*, Mir saheb, peace be with you!" Ghalib greeted his old friend who stood outside his old shop overseeing its renovation.

"*Walekum Assalaam*, Mirza, and peace be with you too," Mir Saheb returned the greeting. "After many months!" He pulled a *moorha* for Ghalib.

"So you finally did think of re-establishing your shop," Ghalib pointed to the shop gutted down in the Mutiny of 1857.

"No, simply getting it repaired," Mir Saheb said. "I cannot bear its burnt look any longer."

"How much does the damage amount to?"

"Ask not, Mirza—there's no account of it. I can estimate the loss of books somehow, but how can I salvage those verses that hadn't graced a book as yet, burnt before they could be printed. Do you have any idea of the number of your verses gutted in the fire?"

"The rashness and imprudence of youth are burnt. Forget it, Mir Saheb. Tell me, do you still get that qahwa here, the one from Palti Darwaza?"

"Yes, yes, it is still available." He shouted for an attendant to fetch some.

The two old men settled down and Ghalib lost himself in the maze of old memories.

"And tell me, how do you keep these days?" Haji Mir asked.

"Age has loosened me, rendered me useless. The legs are in the stirrups, the hands on the reins and a long way to go. There's nothing to meet the expenses on the way, empty-handed do I go," Ghalib answered with his usual fanfare.

The boy arrived with the qahwa and Mir handed a bowl to Ghalib,

"In the last three years," Ghalib said, "I have tasted death everyday. I wonder why I'm still alive. I have lost my senses, cried over my dear ones—and when I get up, I do so in such time that takes a tall wall to be erected. Seventy-one years," he paused to sip his drink, "have I lived. Now life does not seem left in years, I count it by months and days." They both sipped their tea in silence. An *aalaap* on the sarangi from the kotha opposite pierced the silence. They both looked at each other, Ghalib recited:

"Sad jalwa ru bru hai jo musgaan uthaiye
Taqat kahan ke deed ka ahsan uthaiye."

A hundred sights present themselves, you need only lift your eyelids
But where's the strength to lift the gratitude of sight.

They both smiled.

"Hear! Hear! Hear! Every citizen of the city is hereby ordered by Governor General Lord Canning to light up their houses on the night of the first. Decorate the outside of your houses, shops, bazaars. Even the house of the Saheb Commissioner Bahadur will be lit," a man on a *tonga* made the announcement to the accompaniment of beats on the drum.

"Finally, some life and progress seems to be infused in the city," one of the people who gathered to listen to the announcement, said. "Bade Miyan," another commented, "lights do not make a town of dead alive."

"Don't you make that mistake," a third warned, "the Whites will patrol the city at night and if they find not your house lit, you'll be caught."

"Yes, I'll light lamps, in the graveyard where my friends are buried," the second man said bitterly.

6

On the day of the first, the streets and houses were lit, some brightly, others more brightly. Two small earthern lamps burnt in front of Ghalib's house too. British soldiers on mounts patrolled the entire city.

7

Early the next morning at Nanbai's shop, a discussion broke out, before he could even light his oven, when an early bird arrived chewing at his *daatun*.

"The town's still ringing of horses hooves," he said. "They were patrolling through the night, these Whites."

"Was anyone caught?" Nanbai asked. "The city otherwise was lit."

"Yes," the man said. "Many they caught from their homes—in the night itself."

"Is that so?" Nanbai said.

"It was strange the way one acted. He put his house to torch and stood shouting on the street, 'look, you Whites, my entire house is lit.' "

"Who's this man?" Nanbai almost laughed.

"They said he was a Rajput,"

"They must not have done anything to him."

"No. They caught him then and there. That is the strategy of these colourless people. In one go they find out who's with them, who is against." The oven caught fire.

Nanbai asked,

"What did they do to their captives?"

"I've heard that they were hanged at night itself in Mehrauli. They are hanging from trees like nests of birds."

8

A number of bodies hung from trees. Some pyres had been lit to cremate the dead. The place was full of smoke, full of people looking for bodies of their relatives among the dead. Haji Mir's body had been removed from the tree and lay amongst the few scattered dead bodies—two relatives sat beside the corpse. A young boy sat amongst them.

Ghalib, sad and lost, looked at the scene through smoke and turned to go. A few steps away he met Hafiz, the street singer, his clothes tattered. Ghalib removed his shawl and put it on him. The man recognized his touch, "Mirza Nausha?" he asked, "what are you doing here?"

"Bana kar fakiron ka hum bhes Ghalib
Tamasha-e ehl-e karam dekhte hain."

Attorned in the robes of a fakir,
Ghalib, we look at the play of the world.

Hafiz said.

"Are things alright? How are you?"

"Ask not now how I am, Hafiz Miyan," Ghalib answered, "ask my contemporaries a few days later, how I was." He walked away muttring. "I'm tired of life now," he said to himself. "In these years, I've carried so many coffins that when I die, there'll be hardly anyone left to shoulder me."

He walked on, his thoughts ringing in his mind.

"Na tha kuch to khuda tha, kuch na hota to khuda hota
Duboya mujh ko hone ne, na hota main to kya hota"

When nothing existed, there existed God.
I'm let down by my existence.
If I didn't exist, what would I be.

"Hua jab gham se yun behis, to gham kya sar ke katne ka
Na hota gar juda tan se, to zanu par dhara hota."

Having gone immune to pain, why fear the loss of head?
Had it not been separated from the body,
it would have resting on the knees.

He walked on, over the pages of history.

"Hui mudat ke Ghalib mar gaya, par yaad ata hai
Woh har ek baat par kehna, ke yun hota to kya hota."

It is long since Ghalib died, but he is still there in memory.
His arguing at everything, what would it have been,
if it were like this or like that?

Ghalib died two years later. On the fifteenth day of February 1869. He is buried in the graveyard of Loharu dynasty, near Chausath Khamba.

"Ye masail-e tasawuff ye tera bayaan Ghalib
Tujhe hum wali samajhte jo na baadaa-khwaar hota."

Ah Ghalib, the magic of your words and your ways with mystics!
you would have been a saint – if you were not addicted to drink.

"Hu'e mar ke hum jo rusva hu'e kyun na gharqe darya
Na kabhi janaza uthta — na kaheen mazaar hota."

After death I was so digraced; why didn't I just drown in the river?
For then, no coffin had to be raised, nor any grave built.

"Go hathh ko junbish nahin, aankhon mein to dum hai
Rehne dho abhi saaghar – O – meena mere aagay."

"So what if my hands are robbed of the movement,
my eyes still brim with life.
Let the bottles and the glasses be before me."

"Ghar mein tha kya jo tera gham usay gharat karta?
Woh jo hum rakhte the ik hasrat-e tamir, so hai."

*"What did we have at our home that your sorrow could wreck?
All we had was a desire to create, and that is still there."*

"Aur bazaar se le aae agar toot gaya
Saghar-e jam se mera jam-e sifaal achha hai!"

*And you may fetch another if it may be ever broken
This, my earthern goblet, is better than the wine glass of Jamshed.*

"Un ke dekhe se jo aa-jati hai mounh par rounaq
Woh samajhte hain ke beemar ka haal achha hai."

*"And a glow appears on my face when I see her.
She gets the impression that I'm no longer ailing!"*

"Dekhiye pate hain kya faiz buton se ushaq
Ik berhamin ne kaha hai ke ye saal achha hai ."

*Let's see what benefits do I get from idols of love
For a Brahmin has predicted that this year has good things in store.*

"Hum ko maloom hai jannat ki haqeeqat, lekin
Dil ke khush rakhne ko, Ghalib ye khayal achha hai."

And though I know the truth about Paradise
What's the harm if I thus amuse myself.

"Hai ab is mamure mein qahett-e gham-e ulfat Asad
Hum ne yeh maana ki dilli mein rahein khaenge kya?"

There's a dearth in this city of the pangs of unrequited love,
And though I am agreed to stay in Delhi what shall I feed myself on?

"Garcha hai mulke Deccan mein in dinon qadr-e sukhan
kaun jaye Zauq per Dilli ki galliyaan chhor kar!"

Who will now leave these lanes of Dilli
So what if prosperity now camps in the Deccan!

"Naqsh fariyadi hai kis ki shokhi-e tahreer ka
Kaghazi hai pairahan har paikar-e tasweer ka."

These signs are complaint to someone's endearing hand
Papery is the attire of all sizes of pictures.